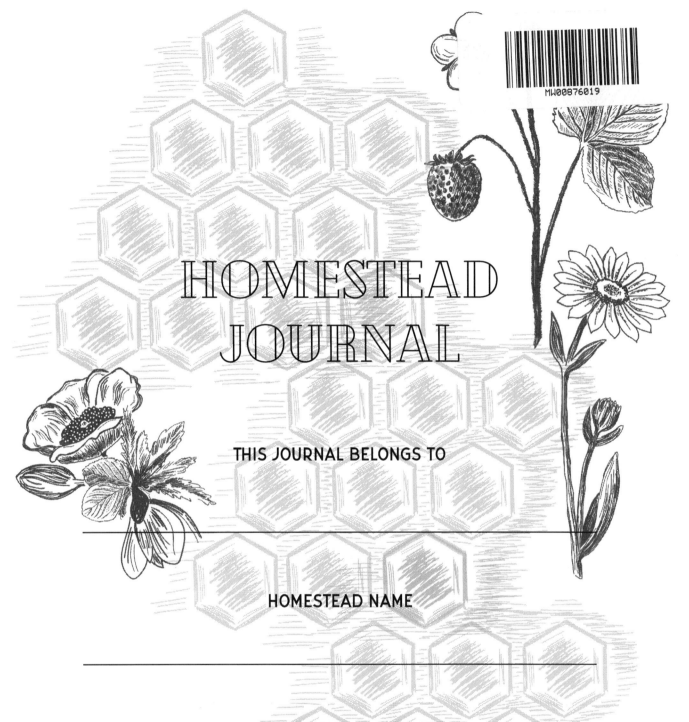

HOMESTEAD JOURNAL

THIS JOURNAL BELONGS TO

_____

HOMESTEAD NAME

_____

IF FOUND, PLEASE CONTACT

_____

HOMESTEAD PLANNER

MONTH:

SUNDAY	MONDAY	TUESDAY	WEDNESDAY

THURSDAY	FRIDAY	SATURDAY	NOTES

MONTH:

SUNDAY	MONDAY	TUESDAY	WEDNESDAY

THURSDAY	FRIDAY	SATURDAY	NOTES

MONTH:

SUNDAY	MONDAY	TUESDAY	WEDNESDAY

THURSDAY	FRIDAY	SATURDAY	NOTES

MONTH:

SUNDAY	MONDAY	TUESDAY	WEDNESDAY

THURSDAY	FRIDAY	SATURDAY	NOTES

MONTH:

SUNDAY	MONDAY	TUESDAY	WEDNESDAY

THURSDAY	FRIDAY	SATURDAY	NOTES

MONTH:

SUNDAY	MONDAY	TUESDAY	WEDNESDAY

THURSDAY	FRIDAY	SATURDAY	NOTES

MONTH:

SUNDAY	MONDAY	TUESDAY	WEDNESDAY

THURSDAY	FRIDAY	SATURDAY	NOTES

MONTH:

SUNDAY	MONDAY	TUESDAY	WEDNESDAY

THURSDAY	FRIDAY	SATURDAY	NOTES

MONTH:

SUNDAY	MONDAY	TUESDAY	WEDNESDAY

THURSDAY	FRIDAY	SATURDAY	NOTES

MONTH:

SUNDAY	MONDAY	TUESDAY	WEDNESDAY

THURSDAY	FRIDAY	SATURDAY	NOTES

MONTH:

SUNDAY	MONDAY	TUESDAY	WEDNESDAY

THURSDAY	FRIDAY	SATURDAY	NOTES

MONTH:

SUNDAY	MONDAY	TUESDAY	WEDNESDAY

THURSDAY	FRIDAY	SATURDAY	NOTES

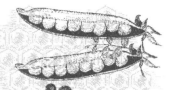

ANNUAL PROJECTS

	REQUIREMENTS	BUDGET

	REQUIREMENTS	BUDGET

	REQUIREMENTS	BUDGET

 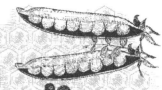

ANNUAL PROJECTS

	REQUIREMENTS	BUDGET

	REQUIREMENTS	BUDGET

	REQUIREMENTS	BUDGET

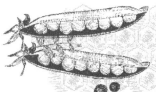 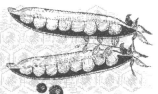

MONTHLY GOALS

JANUARY	FEBRUARY

MARCH	APRIL

MAY	JUNE

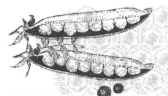

MONTHLY GOALS

JULY

AUGUST

SEPTEMBER

OCTOBER

NOVEMBER

DECEMBER

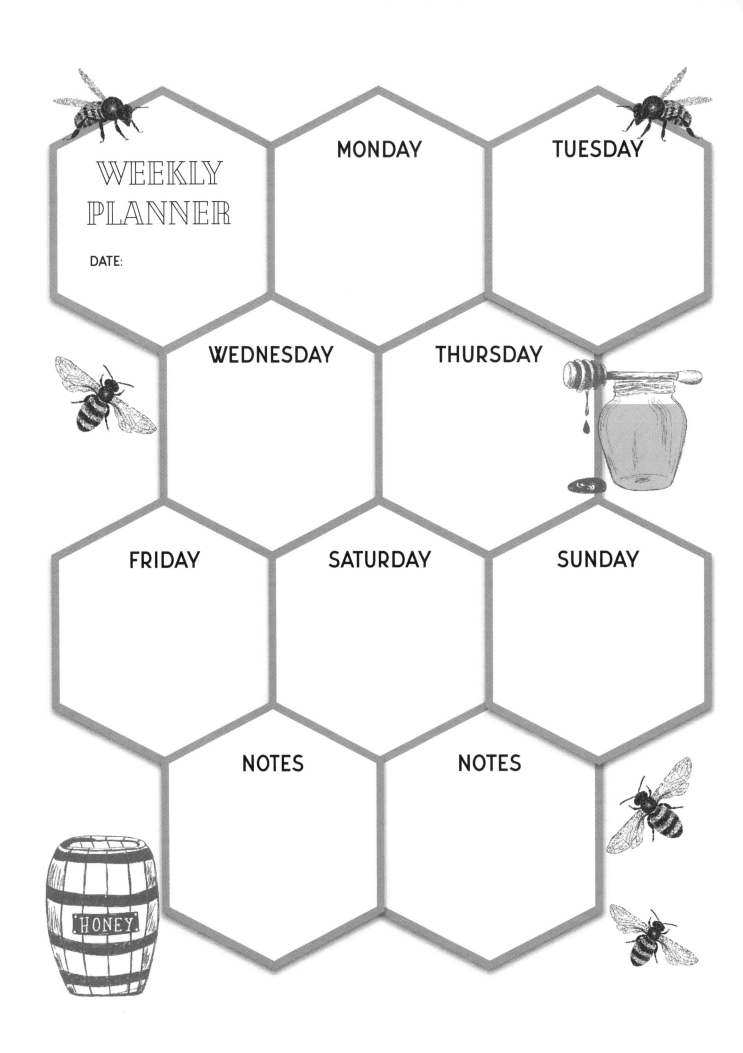

WEEKLY PLANNER

DATE:

MONDAY

TUESDAY

WEDNESDAY

THURSDAY

FRIDAY

SATURDAY

SUNDAY

NOTES

NOTES

CHORES

WEEK:

NAME:

MONDAY

	○
	○
	○
	○
	○
	○

TUESDAY

	○
	○
	○
	○
	○
	○

WEDNESDAY

	○
	○
	○
	○
	○
	○

THURSDAY

	○
	○
	○
	○
	○
	○

FRIDAY

	○
	○
	○
	○
	○
	○

SATURDAY

	○
	○
	○
	○
	○
	○

SUNDAY

	○
	○
	○
	○
	○

NOTES

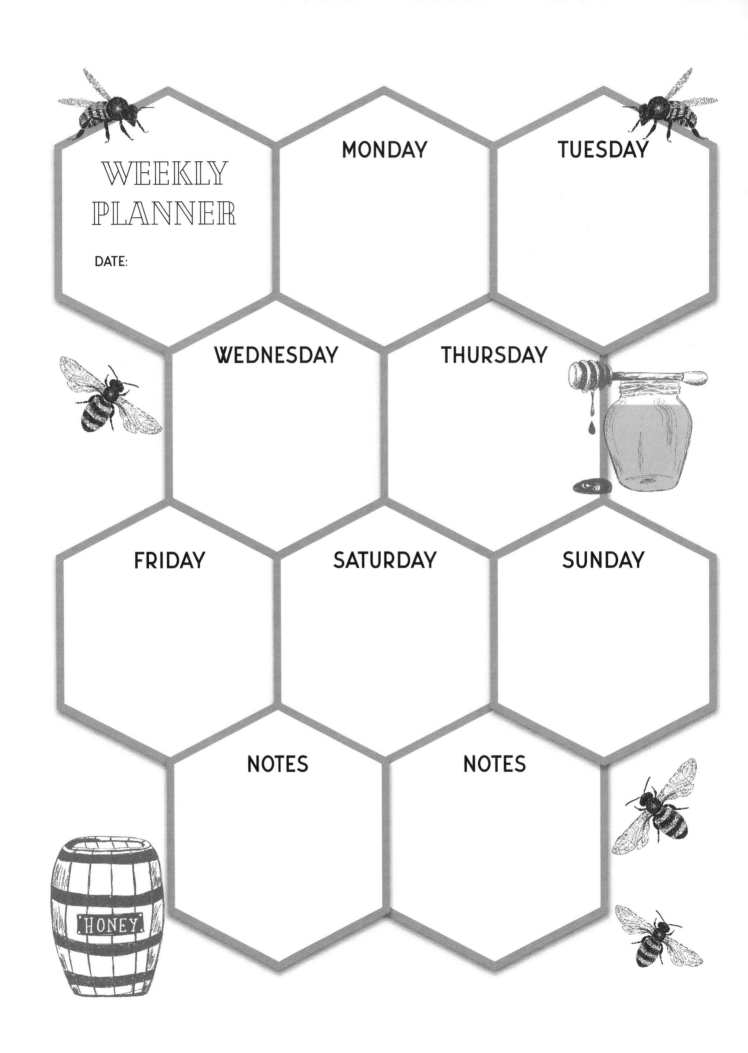

WEEKLY PLANNER

DATE:

MONDAY

TUESDAY

WEDNESDAY

THURSDAY

FRIDAY

SATURDAY

SUNDAY

NOTES

NOTES

HONEY

CHORES

WEEK:

NAME:

MONDAY
- ○
- ○
- ○
- ○
- ○
- ○

TUESDAY
- ○
- ○
- ○
- ○
- ○
- ○

WEDNESDAY
- ○
- ○
- ○
- ○
- ○
- ○

THURSDAY
- ○
- ○
- ○
- ○
- ○
- ○

FRIDAY
- ○
- ○
- ○
- ○
- ○
- ○

SATURDAY
- ○
- ○
- ○
- ○
- ○
- ○

SUNDAY
- ○
- ○
- ○
- ○
- ○

NOTES

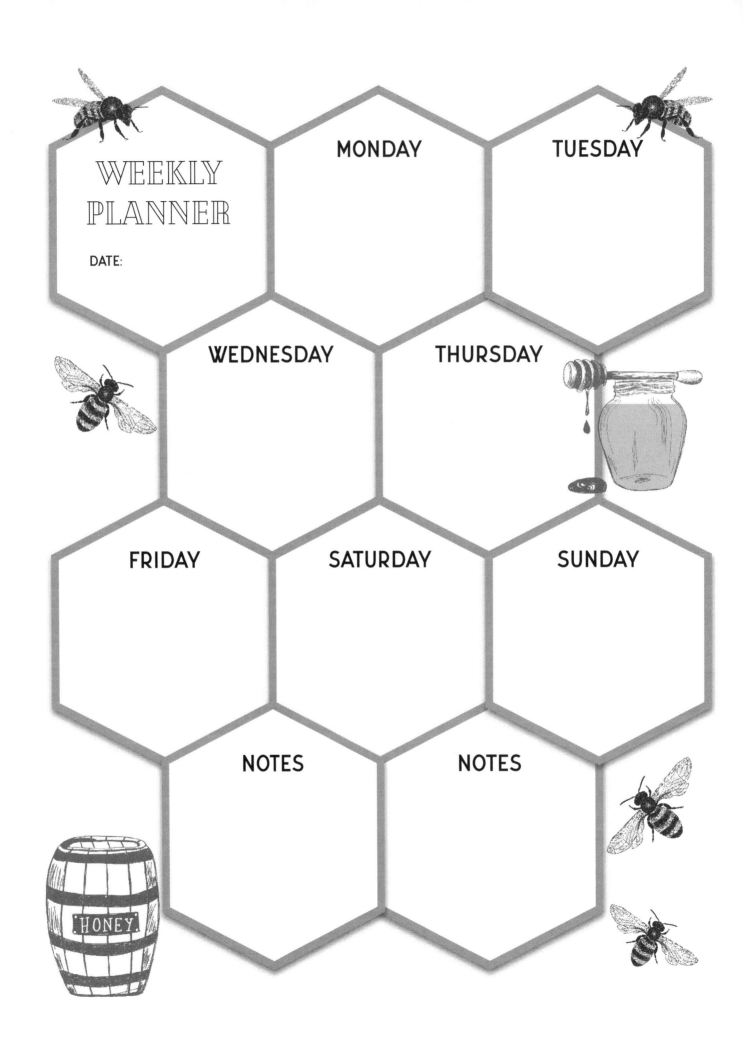

WEEKLY PLANNER

DATE:

MONDAY

TUESDAY

WEDNESDAY

THURSDAY

FRIDAY

SATURDAY

SUNDAY

NOTES

NOTES

CHORES

WEEK:

NAME:

MONDAY

	○
	○
	○
	○
	○
	○

TUESDAY

	○
	○
	○
	○
	○
	○

WEDNESDAY

	○
	○
	○
	○
	○
	○

THURSDAY

	○
	○
	○
	○
	○
	○

FRIDAY

	○
	○
	○
	○
	○
	○

SATURDAY

	○
	○
	○
	○
	○
	○

SUNDAY

	○
	○
	○
	○
	○

NOTES

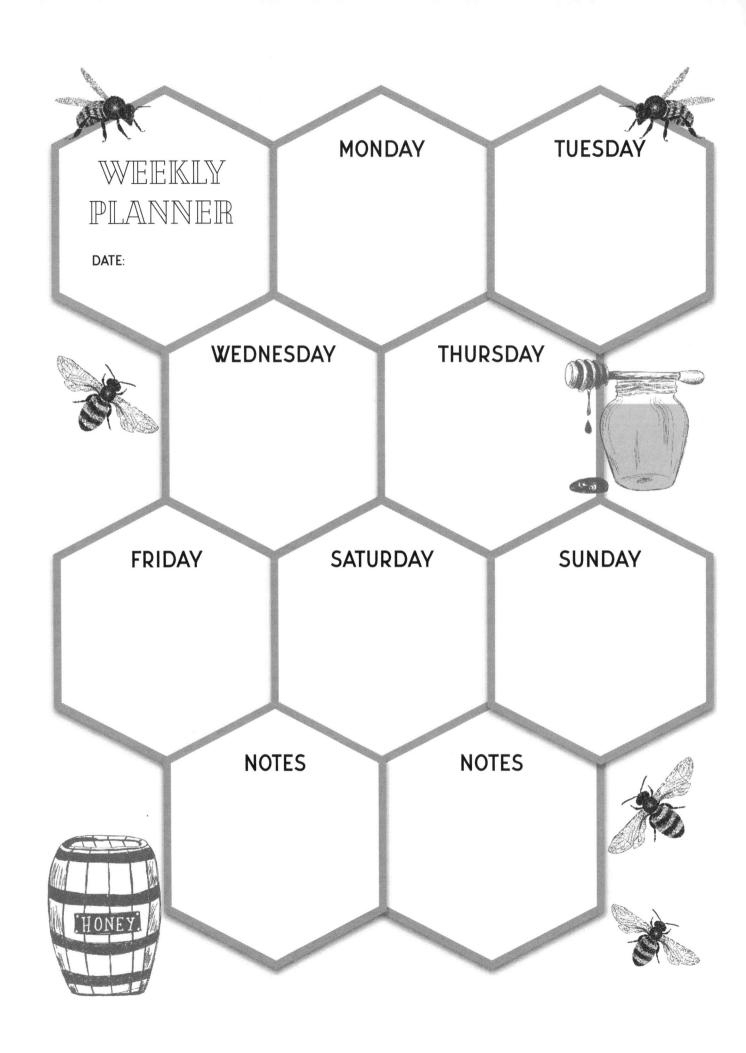

WEEKLY PLANNER

DATE:

MONDAY

TUESDAY

WEDNESDAY

THURSDAY

FRIDAY

SATURDAY

SUNDAY

NOTES

NOTES

HONEY

CHORES

MONDAY

- ○
- ○
- ○
- ○
- ○
- ○

TUESDAY

- ○
- ○
- ○
- ○
- ○
- ○

WEDNESDAY

- ○
- ○
- ○
- ○
- ○
- ○

THURSDAY

- ○
- ○
- ○
- ○
- ○
- ○

FRIDAY

- ○
- ○
- ○
- ○
- ○
- ○

SATURDAY

- ○
- ○
- ○
- ○
- ○
- ○

SUNDAY

- ○
- ○
- ○
- ○
- ○

NOTES

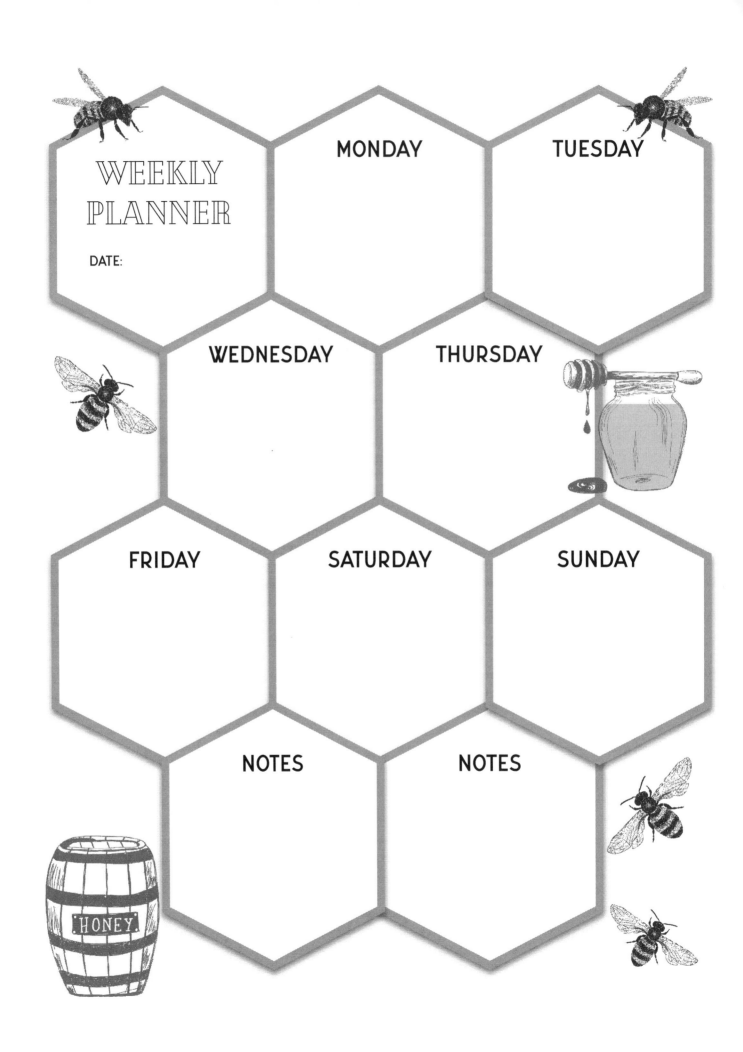

WEEKLY PLANNER

DATE:

MONDAY

TUESDAY

WEDNESDAY

THURSDAY

FRIDAY

SATURDAY

SUNDAY

NOTES

NOTES

HONEY

CHORES

WEEK:

NAME:

MONDAY

○
○
○
○
○
○

TUESDAY

○
○
○
○
○
○

WEDNESDAY

○
○
○
○
○
○

THURSDAY

○
○
○
○
○
○

FRIDAY

○
○
○
○
○
○

SATURDAY

○
○
○
○
○
○

SUNDAY

○
○
○
○
○

NOTES

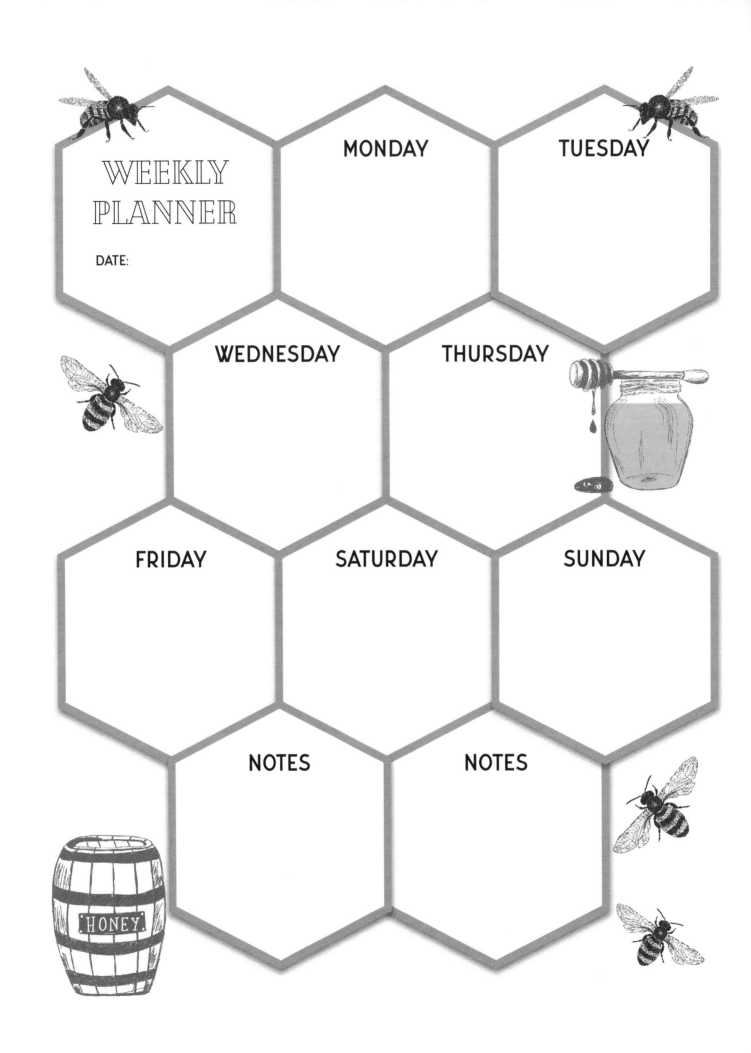

WEEKLY PLANNER

DATE:

MONDAY

TUESDAY

WEDNESDAY

THURSDAY

FRIDAY

SATURDAY

SUNDAY

NOTES

NOTES

CHORES

WEEK:

NAME:

MONDAY

	○
	○
	○
	○
	○
	○

TUESDAY

	○
	○
	○
	○
	○
	○

WEDNESDAY

	○
	○
	○
	○
	○
	○

THURSDAY

	○
	○
	○
	○
	○
	○

FRIDAY

	○
	○
	○
	○
	○
	○

SATURDAY

	○
	○
	○
	○
	○
	○

SUNDAY

	○
	○
	○
	○
	○

NOTES

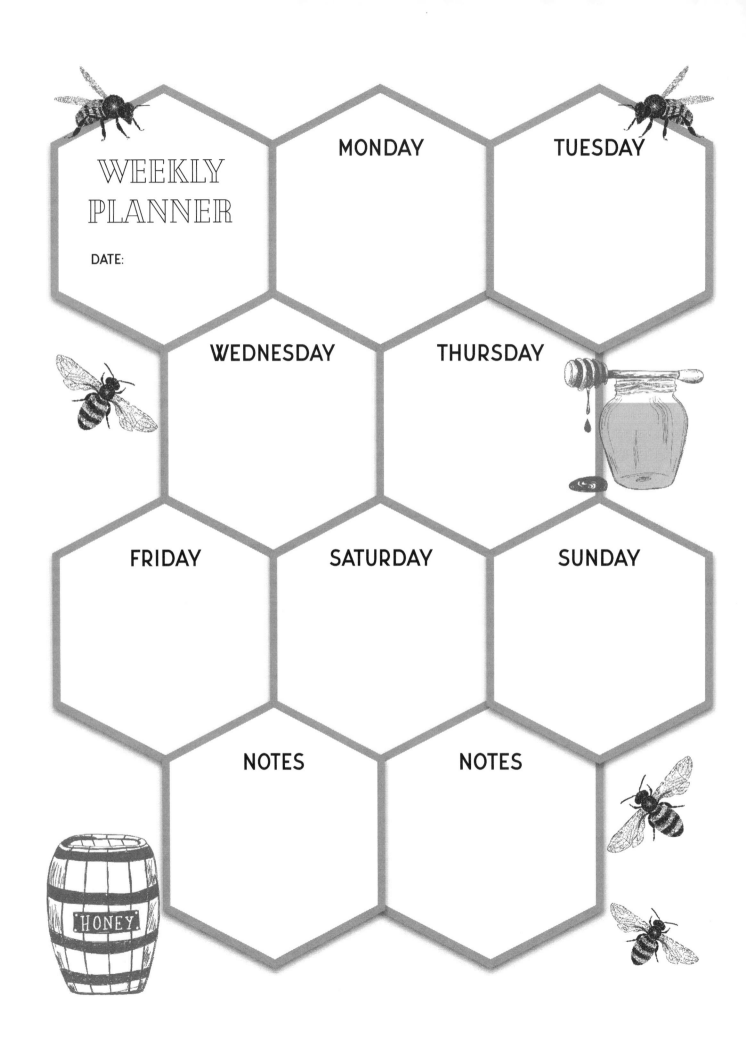

WEEKLY PLANNER

DATE:

MONDAY

TUESDAY

WEDNESDAY

THURSDAY

FRIDAY

SATURDAY

SUNDAY

NOTES

NOTES

CHORES

MONDAY

	○
	○
	○
	○
	○
	○

TUESDAY

	○
	○
	○
	○
	○
	○

WEDNESDAY

	○
	○
	○
	○
	○
	○

THURSDAY

	○
	○
	○
	○
	○
	○

FRIDAY

	○
	○
	○
	○
	○
	○

SATURDAY

	○
	○
	○
	○
	○
	○

SUNDAY

	○
	○
	○
	○
	○

NOTES

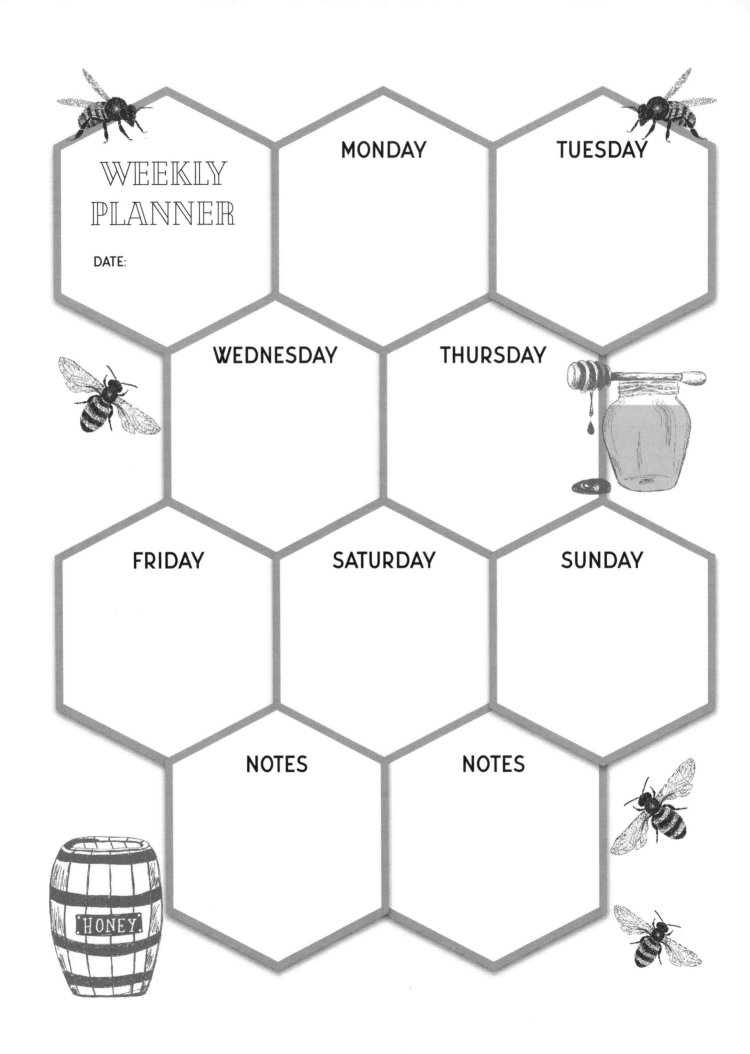

WEEKLY PLANNER

DATE:

MONDAY

TUESDAY

WEDNESDAY

THURSDAY

FRIDAY

SATURDAY

SUNDAY

NOTES

NOTES

HONEY

CHORES

WEEK:

NAME:

MONDAY
- ○
- ○
- ○
- ○
- ○
- ○

TUESDAY
- ○
- ○
- ○
- ○
- ○
- ○

WEDNESDAY
- ○
- ○
- ○
- ○
- ○
- ○

THURSDAY
- ○
- ○
- ○
- ○
- ○
- ○

FRIDAY
- ○
- ○
- ○
- ○
- ○
- ○

SATURDAY
- ○
- ○
- ○
- ○
- ○
- ○

SUNDAY
- ○
- ○
- ○
- ○
- ○

NOTES

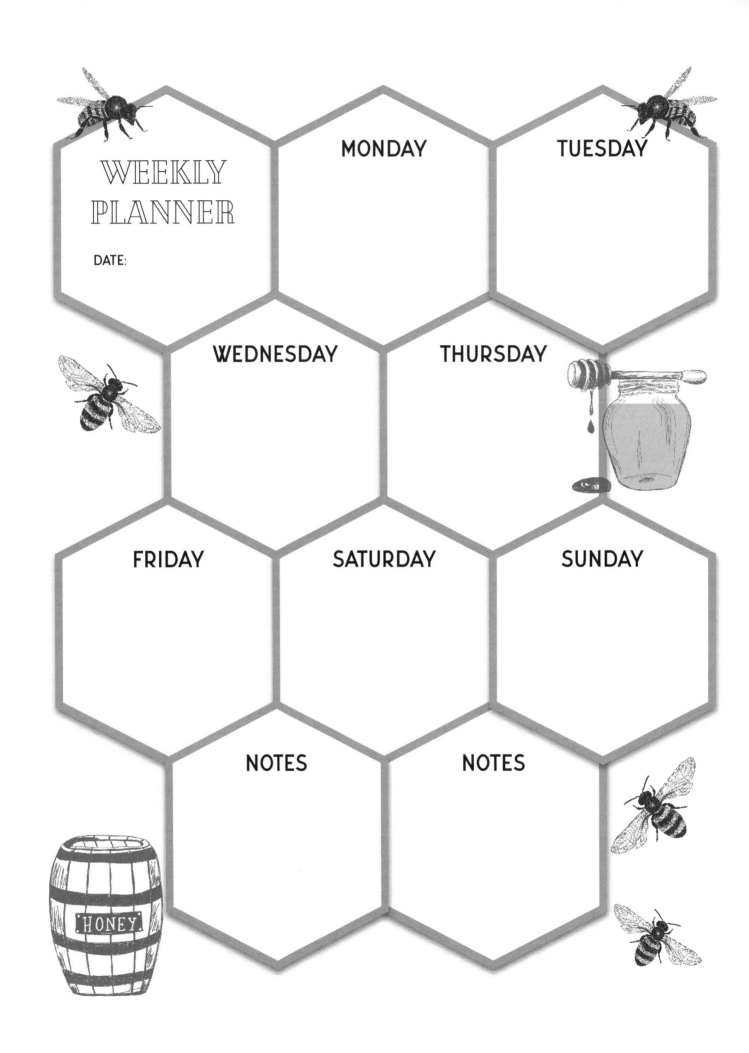

WEEKLY PLANNER

DATE:

MONDAY

TUESDAY

WEDNESDAY

THURSDAY

FRIDAY

SATURDAY

SUNDAY

NOTES

NOTES

HONEY

CHORES

WEEK:

NAME:

MONDAY	
	○
	○
	○
	○
	○
	○

TUESDAY	
	○
	○
	○
	○
	○
	○

WEDNESDAY	
	○
	○
	○
	○
	○
	○

THURSDAY	
	○
	○
	○
	○
	○
	○

FRIDAY	
	○
	○
	○
	○
	○
	○

SATURDAY	
	○
	○
	○
	○
	○
	○

SUNDAY	
	○
	○
	○
	○
	○

NOTES

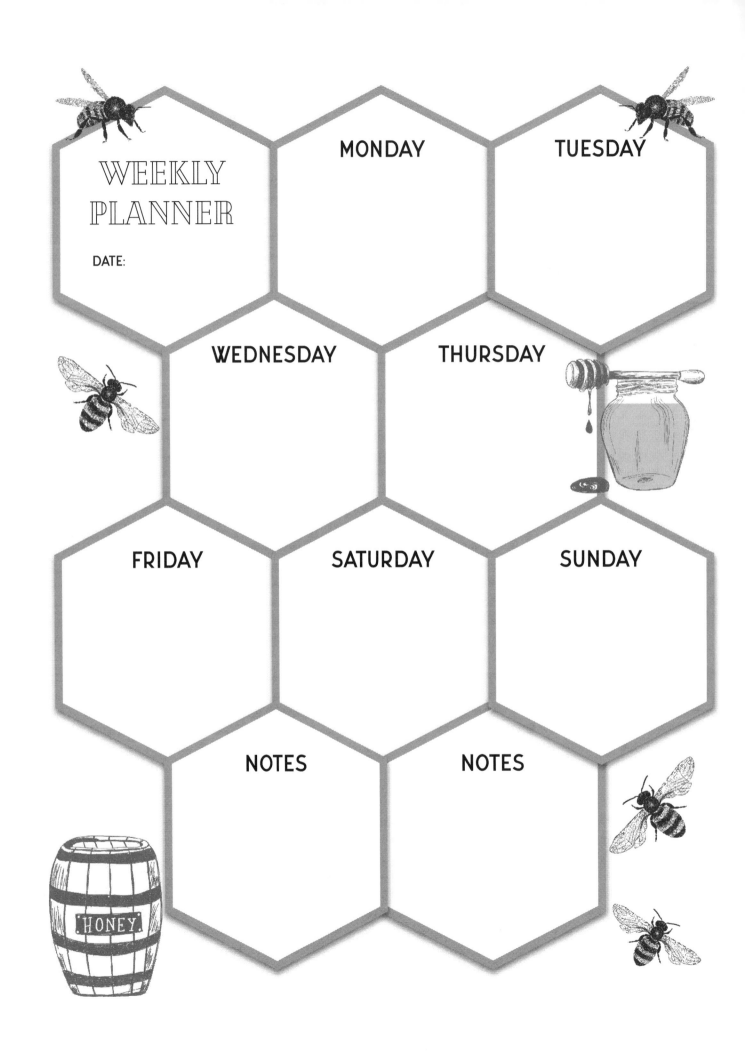

WEEKLY PLANNER

DATE:

MONDAY

TUESDAY

WEDNESDAY

THURSDAY

FRIDAY

SATURDAY

SUNDAY

NOTES

NOTES

HONEY.

CHORES

WEEK:

NAME:

MONDAY
- ○
- ○
- ○
- ○
- ○
- ○

TUESDAY
- ○
- ○
- ○
- ○
- ○
- ○

WEDNESDAY
- ○
- ○
- ○
- ○
- ○
- ○

THURSDAY
- ○
- ○
- ○
- ○
- ○
- ○

FRIDAY
- ○
- ○
- ○
- ○
- ○
- ○

SATURDAY
- ○
- ○
- ○
- ○
- ○
- ○

SUNDAY
- ○
- ○
- ○
- ○
- ○

NOTES

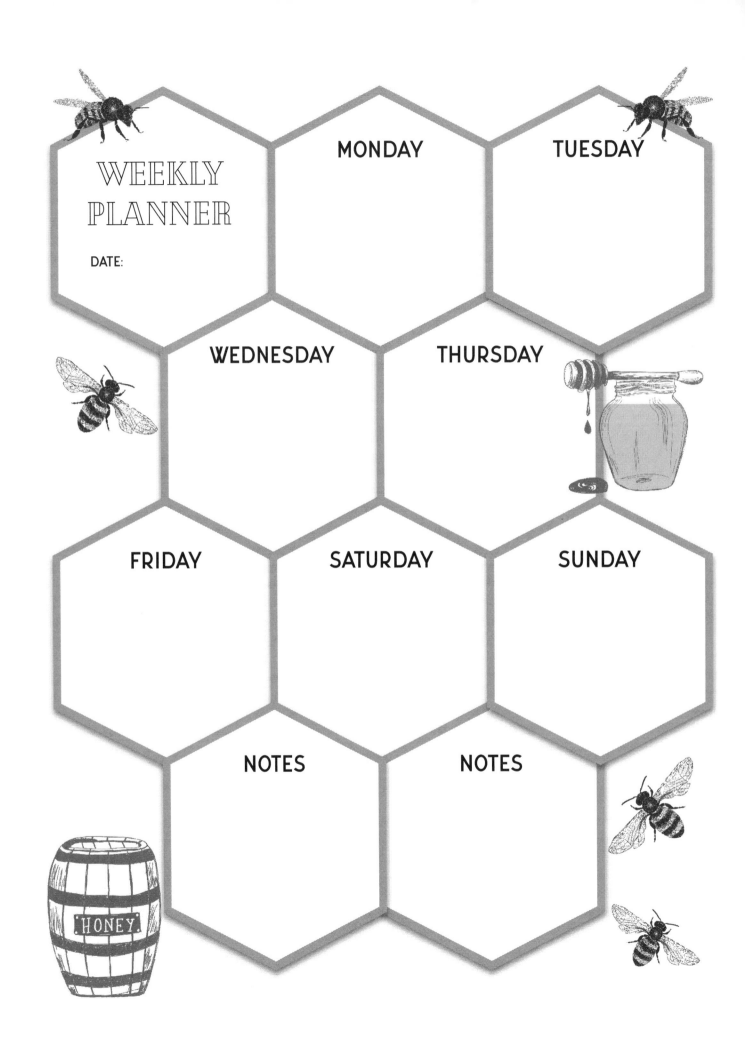

WEEKLY PLANNER

DATE:

MONDAY

TUESDAY

WEDNESDAY

THURSDAY

FRIDAY

SATURDAY

SUNDAY

NOTES

NOTES

HONEY

CHORES

WEEK:

NAME:

MONDAY

	○
	○
	○
	○
	○
	○

TUESDAY

	○
	○
	○
	○
	○
	○

WEDNESDAY

	○
	○
	○
	○
	○
	○

THURSDAY

	○
	○
	○
	○
	○
	○

FRIDAY

	○
	○
	○
	○
	○
	○

SATURDAY

	○
	○
	○
	○
	○
	○

SUNDAY

	○
	○
	○
	○
	○

NOTES

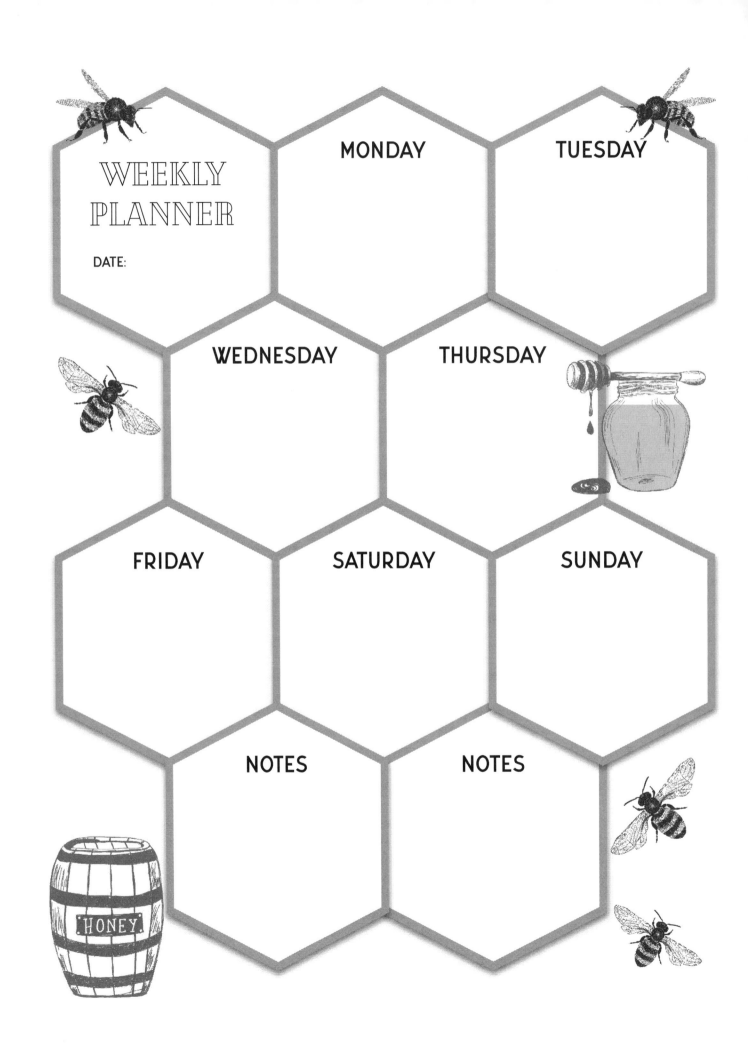

WEEKLY PLANNER

DATE:

MONDAY

TUESDAY

WEDNESDAY

THURSDAY

FRIDAY

SATURDAY

SUNDAY

NOTES

NOTES

CHORES

WEEK:

NAME:

MONDAY

- ○
- ○
- ○
- ○
- ○
- ○

TUESDAY

- ○
- ○
- ○
- ○
- ○
- ○

WEDNESDAY

- ○
- ○
- ○
- ○
- ○
- ○

THURSDAY

- ○
- ○
- ○
- ○
- ○
- ○

FRIDAY

- ○
- ○
- ○
- ○
- ○
- ○

SATURDAY

- ○
- ○
- ○
- ○
- ○
- ○

SUNDAY

- ○
- ○
- ○
- ○
- ○

NOTES

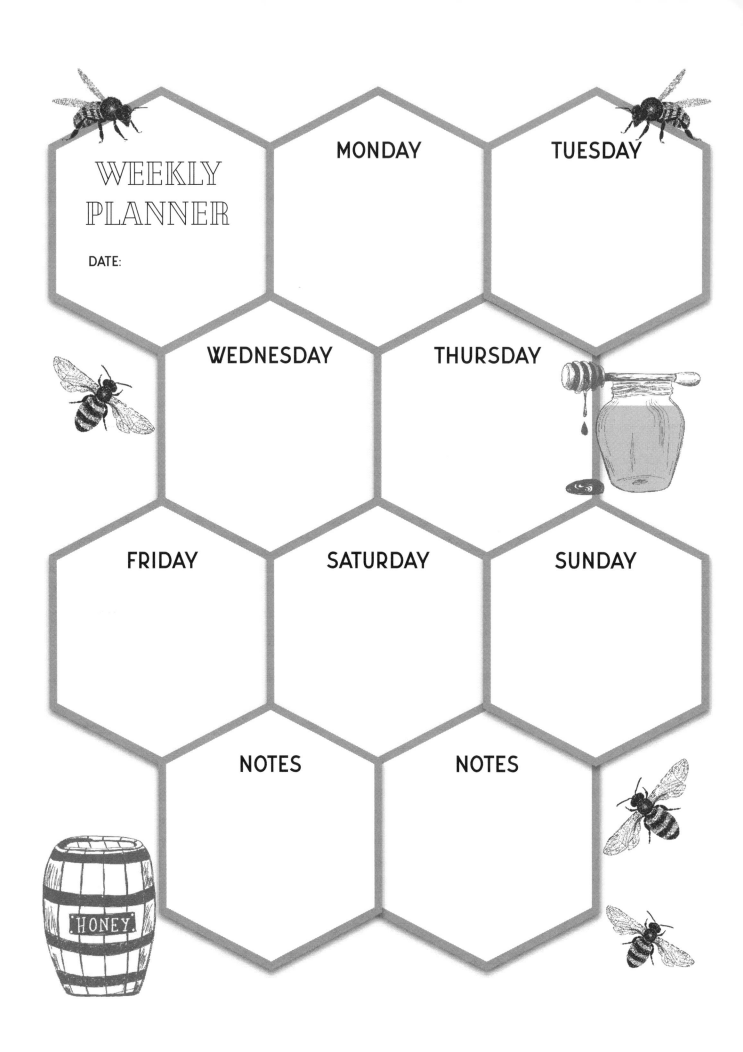

WEEKLY PLANNER

DATE:

MONDAY

TUESDAY

WEDNESDAY

THURSDAY

FRIDAY

SATURDAY

SUNDAY

NOTES

NOTES

HONEY

CHORES

WEEK:

NAME:

MONDAY
- ○
- ○
- ○
- ○
- ○
- ○

TUESDAY
- ○
- ○
- ○
- ○
- ○
- ○

WEDNESDAY
- ○
- ○
- ○
- ○
- ○
- ○

THURSDAY
- ○
- ○
- ○
- ○
- ○
- ○

FRIDAY
- ○
- ○
- ○
- ○
- ○
- ○

SATURDAY
- ○
- ○
- ○
- ○
- ○
- ○

SUNDAY
- ○
- ○
- ○
- ○
- ○

NOTES

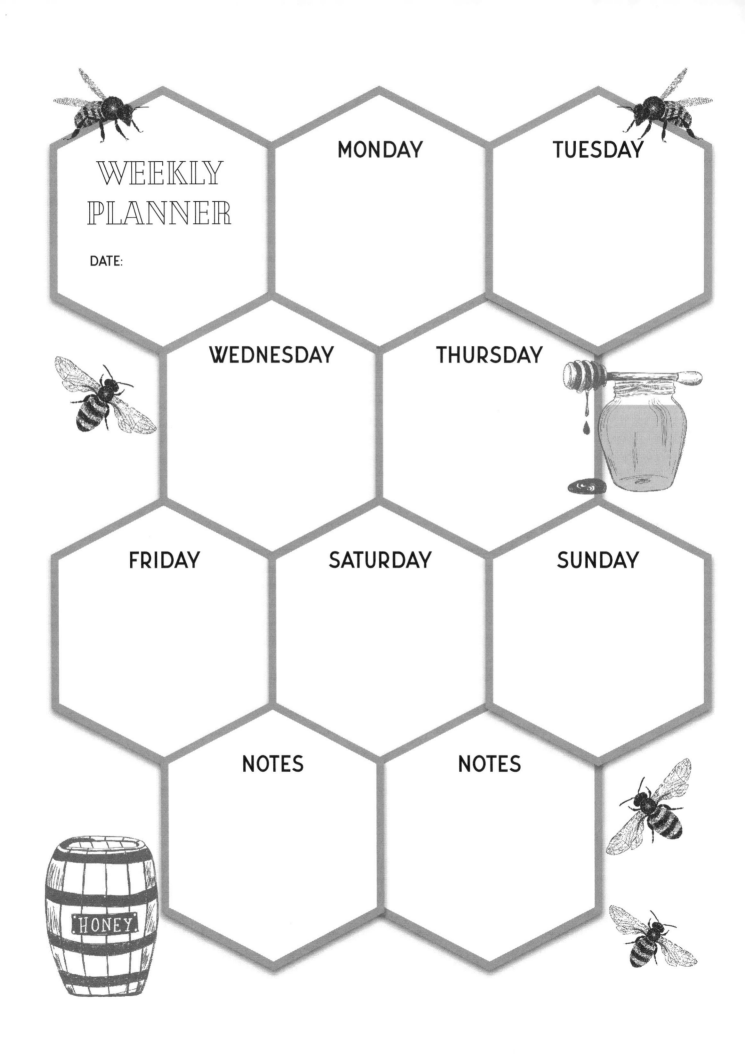

WEEKLY PLANNER

DATE:

MONDAY

TUESDAY

WEDNESDAY

THURSDAY

FRIDAY

SATURDAY

SUNDAY

NOTES

NOTES

HONEY

CHORES

WEEK:

NAME:

MONDAY

- ○
- ○
- ○
- ○
- ○
- ○

TUESDAY

- ○
- ○
- ○
- ○
- ○
- ○

WEDNESDAY

- ○
- ○
- ○
- ○
- ○
- ○

THURSDAY

- ○
- ○
- ○
- ○
- ○
- ○

FRIDAY

- ○
- ○
- ○
- ○
- ○
- ○

SATURDAY

- ○
- ○
- ○
- ○
- ○
- ○

SUNDAY

- ○
- ○
- ○
- ○
- ○

NOTES

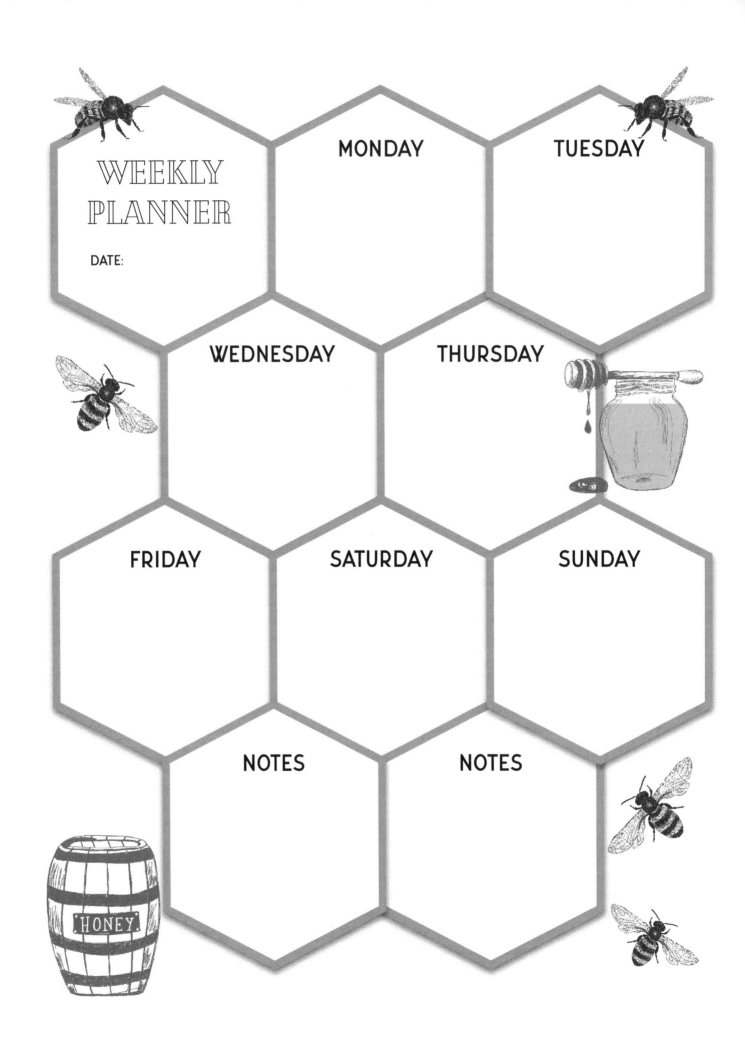

WEEKLY PLANNER

DATE:

MONDAY

TUESDAY

WEDNESDAY

THURSDAY

FRIDAY

SATURDAY

SUNDAY

NOTES

NOTES

HONEY

CHORES

WEEK:

NAME:

MONDAY

- ○
- ○
- ○
- ○
- ○
- ○

TUESDAY

- ○
- ○
- ○
- ○
- ○
- ○

WEDNESDAY

- ○
- ○
- ○
- ○
- ○
- ○

THURSDAY

- ○
- ○
- ○
- ○
- ○
- ○

FRIDAY

- ○
- ○
- ○
- ○
- ○
- ○

SATURDAY

- ○
- ○
- ○
- ○
- ○
- ○

SUNDAY

- ○
- ○
- ○
- ○
- ○

NOTES

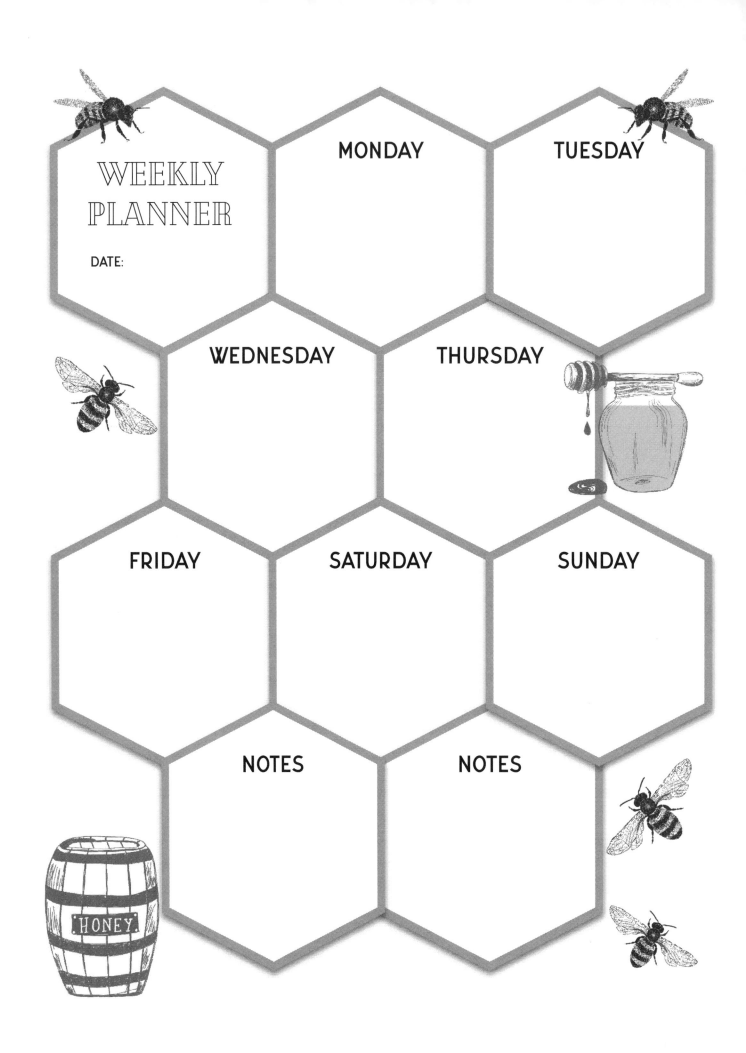

WEEKLY PLANNER

DATE:

MONDAY

TUESDAY

WEDNESDAY

THURSDAY

FRIDAY

SATURDAY

SUNDAY

NOTES

NOTES

HONEY

CHORES

WEEK:

NAME:

MONDAY

	○
	○
	○
	○
	○
	○

TUESDAY

	○
	○
	○
	○
	○
	○

WEDNESDAY

	○
	○
	○
	○
	○
	○

THURSDAY

	○
	○
	○
	○
	○
	○

FRIDAY

	○
	○
	○
	○
	○
	○

SATURDAY

	○
	○
	○
	○
	○
	○

SUNDAY

	○
	○
	○
	○
	○

NOTES

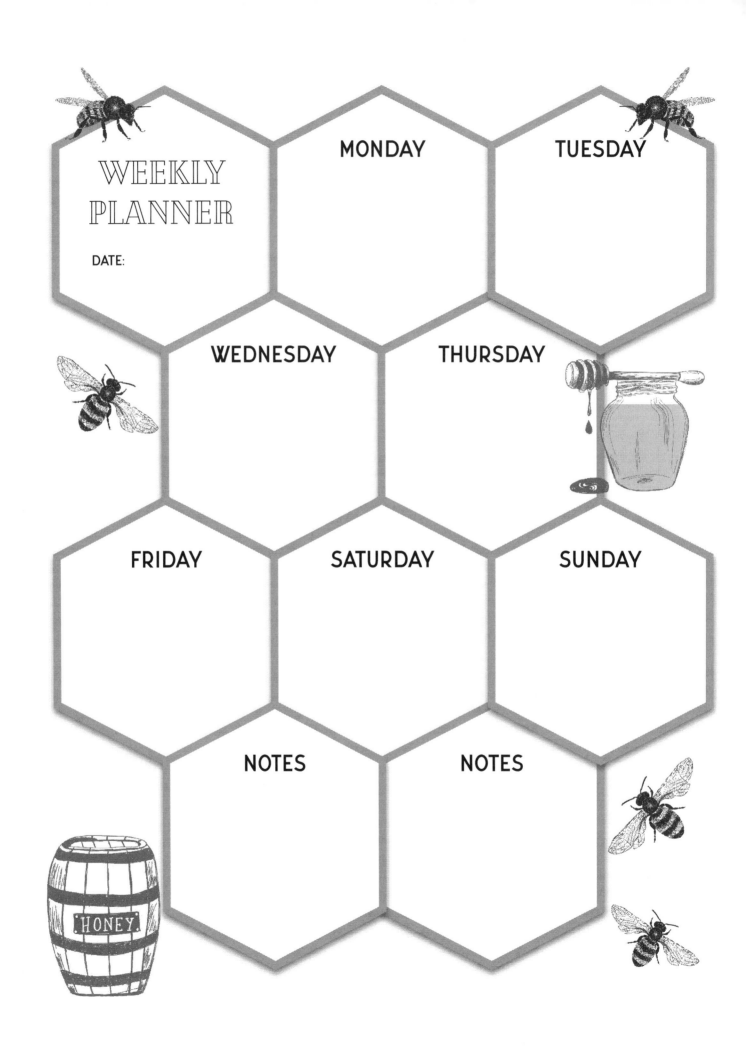

WEEKLY PLANNER

DATE:

MONDAY

TUESDAY

WEDNESDAY

THURSDAY

FRIDAY

SATURDAY

SUNDAY

NOTES

NOTES

HONEY

CHORES

MONDAY

	○
	○
	○
	○
	○
	○

TUESDAY

	○
	○
	○
	○
	○
	○

WEDNESDAY

	○
	○
	○
	○
	○
	○

THURSDAY

	○
	○
	○
	○
	○
	○

FRIDAY

	○
	○
	○
	○
	○
	○

SATURDAY

	○
	○
	○
	○
	○
	○

SUNDAY

	○
	○
	○
	○
	○

NOTES

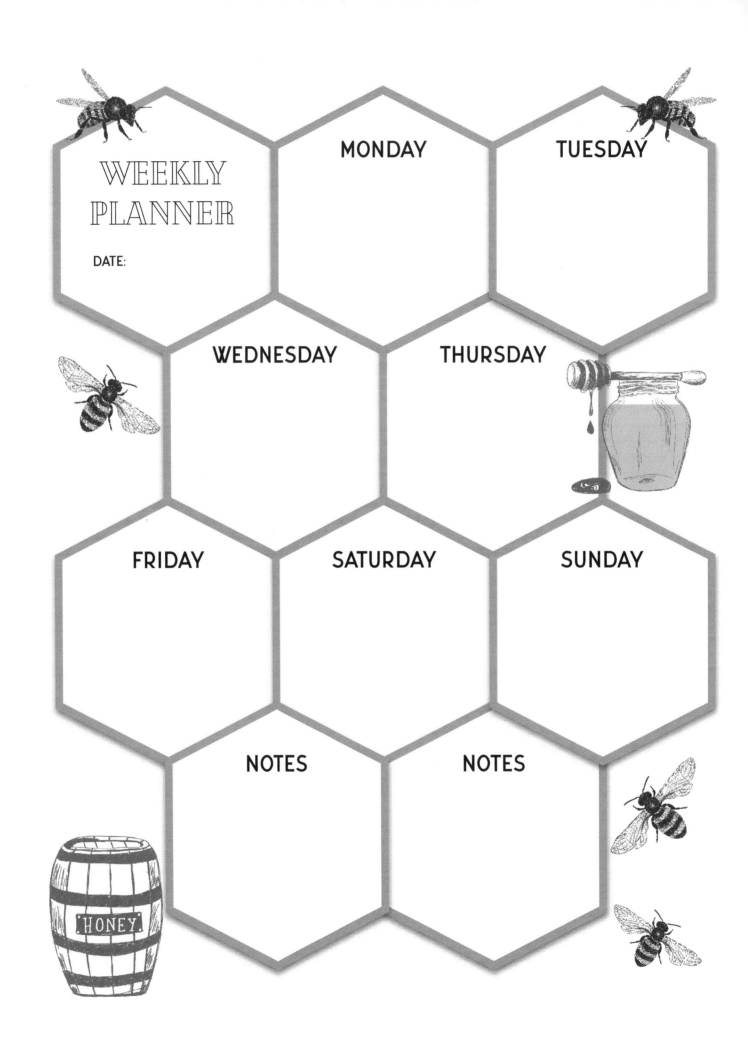

WEEKLY PLANNER

DATE:

MONDAY

TUESDAY

WEDNESDAY

THURSDAY

FRIDAY

SATURDAY

SUNDAY

NOTES

NOTES

HONEY

CHORES

WEEK:

NAME:

MONDAY
- ○
- ○
- ○
- ○
- ○
- ○

TUESDAY
- ○
- ○
- ○
- ○
- ○
- ○

WEDNESDAY
- ○
- ○
- ○
- ○
- ○
- ○

THURSDAY
- ○
- ○
- ○
- ○
- ○
- ○

FRIDAY
- ○
- ○
- ○
- ○
- ○
- ○

SATURDAY
- ○
- ○
- ○
- ○
- ○
- ○

SUNDAY
- ○
- ○
- ○
- ○
- ○

NOTES

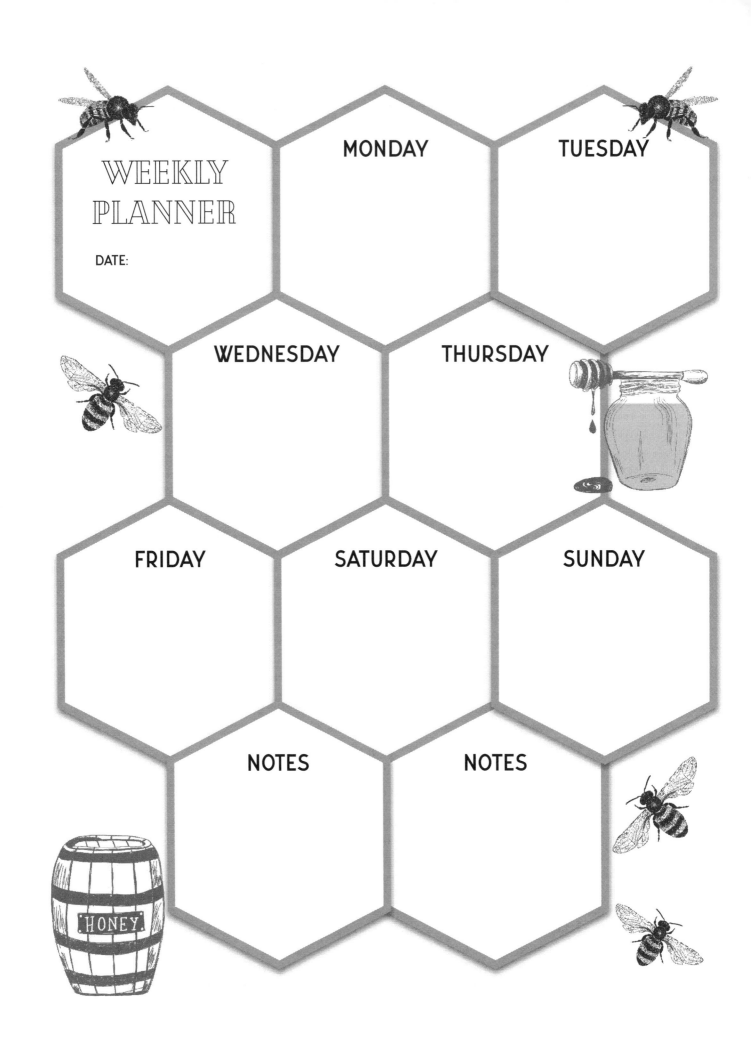

WEEKLY PLANNER

DATE:

MONDAY

TUESDAY

WEDNESDAY

THURSDAY

FRIDAY

SATURDAY

SUNDAY

NOTES

NOTES

HONEY

CHORES

WEEK:

NAME:

MONDAY

	○
	○
	○
	○
	○
	○

TUESDAY

	○
	○
	○
	○
	○
	○

WEDNESDAY

	○
	○
	○
	○
	○
	○

THURSDAY

	○
	○
	○
	○
	○
	○

FRIDAY

	○
	○
	○
	○
	○
	○

SATURDAY

	○
	○
	○
	○
	○
	○

SUNDAY

	○
	○
	○
	○
	○

NOTES

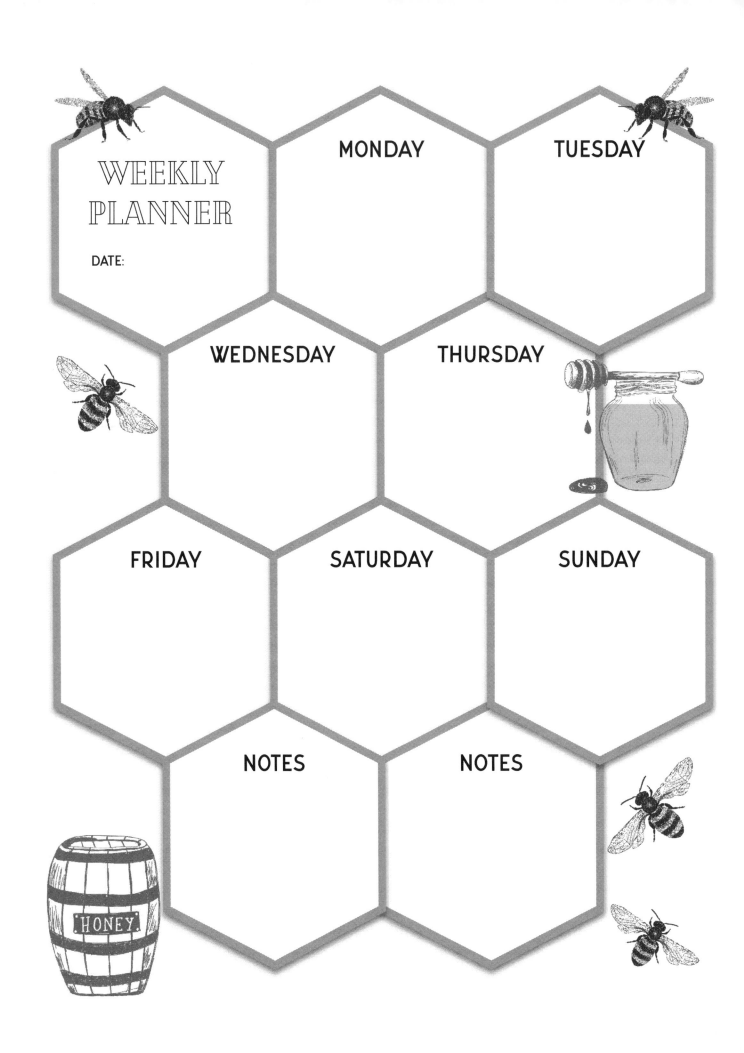

WEEKLY PLANNER

DATE:

MONDAY

TUESDAY

WEDNESDAY

THURSDAY

FRIDAY

SATURDAY

SUNDAY

NOTES

NOTES

CHORES

WEEK:

NAME:

MONDAY

	○
	○
	○
	○
	○
	○

TUESDAY

	○
	○
	○
	○
	○
	○

WEDNESDAY

	○
	○
	○
	○
	○
	○

THURSDAY

	○
	○
	○
	○
	○
	○

FRIDAY

	○
	○
	○
	○
	○
	○

SATURDAY

	○
	○
	○
	○
	○
	○

SUNDAY

	○
	○
	○
	○
	○

NOTES

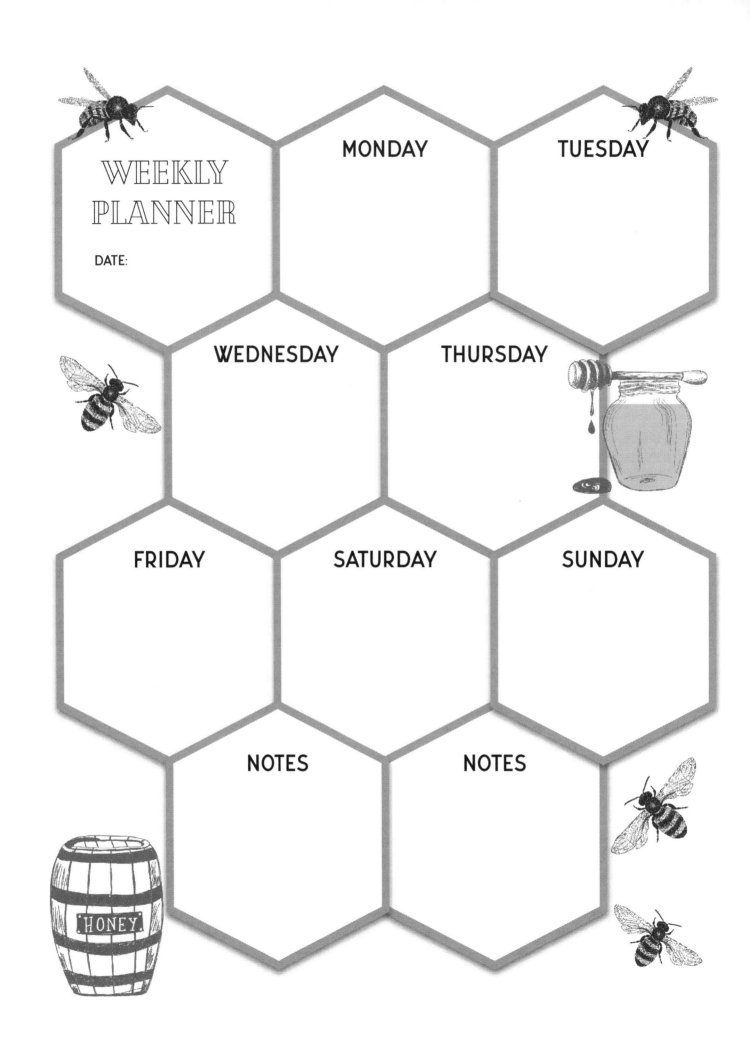

WEEKLY PLANNER

DATE:

MONDAY

TUESDAY

WEDNESDAY

THURSDAY

FRIDAY

SATURDAY

SUNDAY

NOTES

NOTES

HONEY

CHORES

MONDAY
- ○
- ○
- ○
- ○
- ○
- ○

TUESDAY
- ○
- ○
- ○
- ○
- ○
- ○

WEDNESDAY
- ○
- ○
- ○
- ○
- ○
- ○

THURSDAY
- ○
- ○
- ○
- ○
- ○
- ○

FRIDAY
- ○
- ○
- ○
- ○
- ○
- ○

SATURDAY
- ○
- ○
- ○
- ○
- ○

SUNDAY
- ○
- ○
- ○
- ○
- ○

NOTES

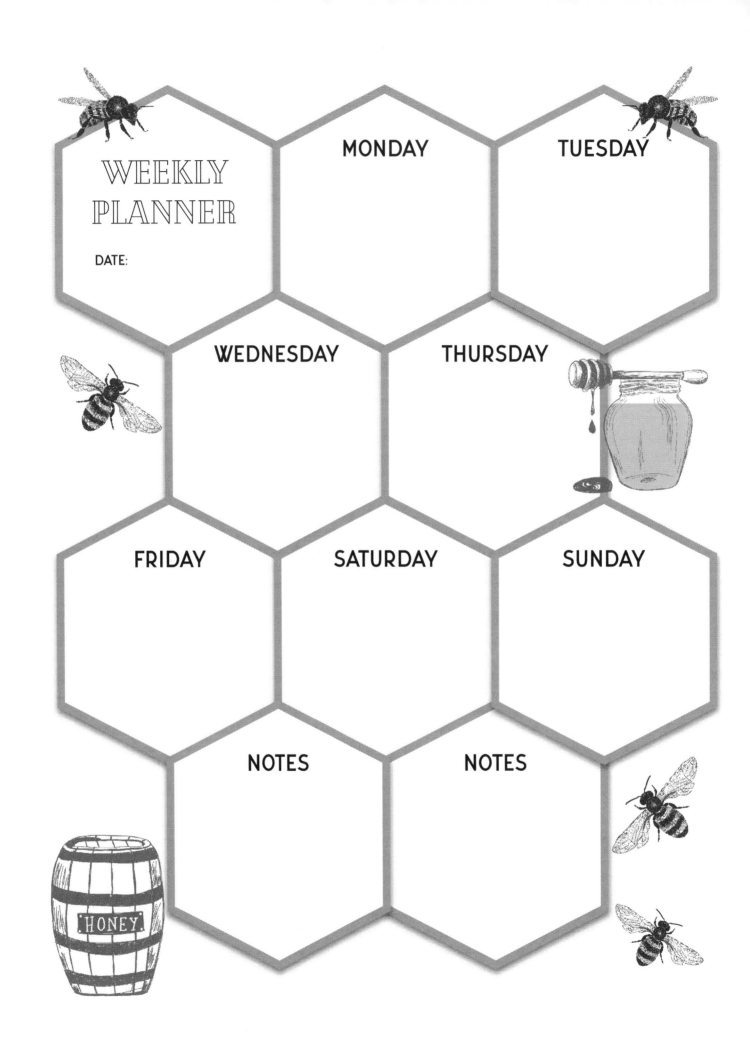

CHORES

WEEK:

NAME:

MONDAY

- ○
- ○
- ○
- ○
- ○
- ○

TUESDAY

- ○
- ○
- ○
- ○
- ○
- ○

WEDNESDAY

- ○
- ○
- ○
- ○
- ○
- ○

THURSDAY

- ○
- ○
- ○
- ○
- ○
- ○

FRIDAY

- ○
- ○
- ○
- ○
- ○
- ○

SATURDAY

- ○
- ○
- ○
- ○
- ○
- ○

SUNDAY

- ○
- ○
- ○
- ○
- ○

NOTES

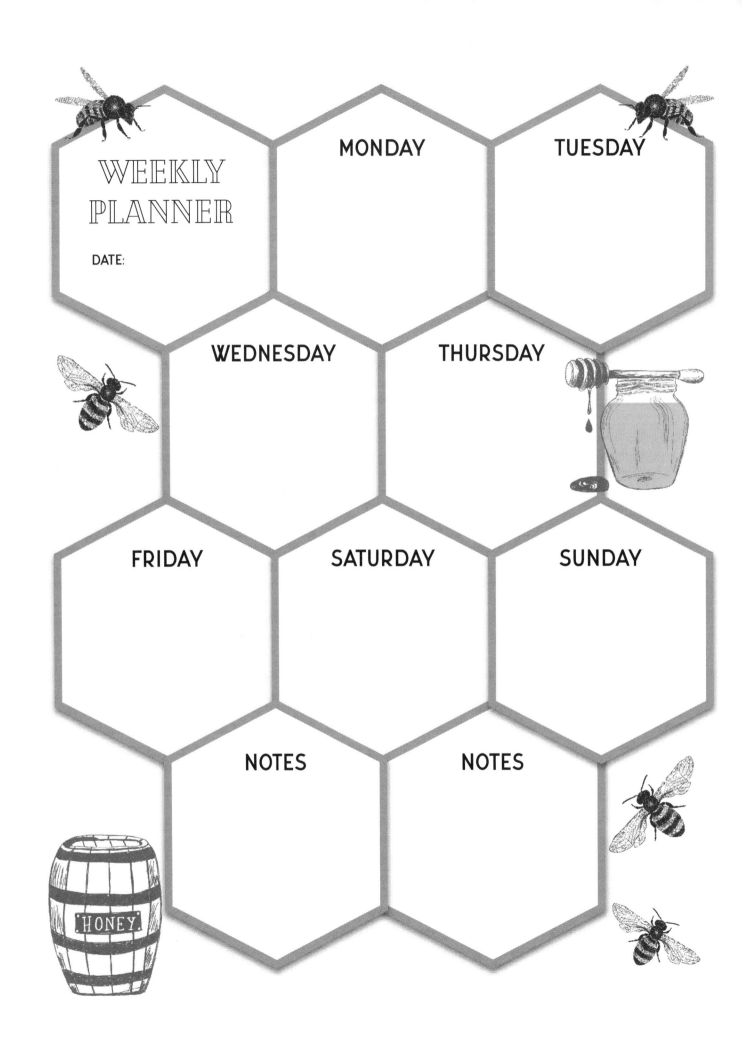

WEEKLY PLANNER

DATE:

MONDAY

TUESDAY

WEDNESDAY

THURSDAY

FRIDAY

SATURDAY

SUNDAY

NOTES

NOTES

HONEY

CHORES

WEEK:

NAME:

MONDAY

- ○
- ○
- ○
- ○
- ○
- ○

TUESDAY

- ○
- ○
- ○
- ○
- ○
- ○

WEDNESDAY

- ○
- ○
- ○
- ○
- ○
- ○

THURSDAY

- ○
- ○
- ○
- ○
- ○
- ○

FRIDAY

- ○
- ○
- ○
- ○
- ○
- ○

SATURDAY

- ○
- ○
- ○
- ○
- ○
- ○

SUNDAY

- ○
- ○
- ○
- ○
- ○

NOTES

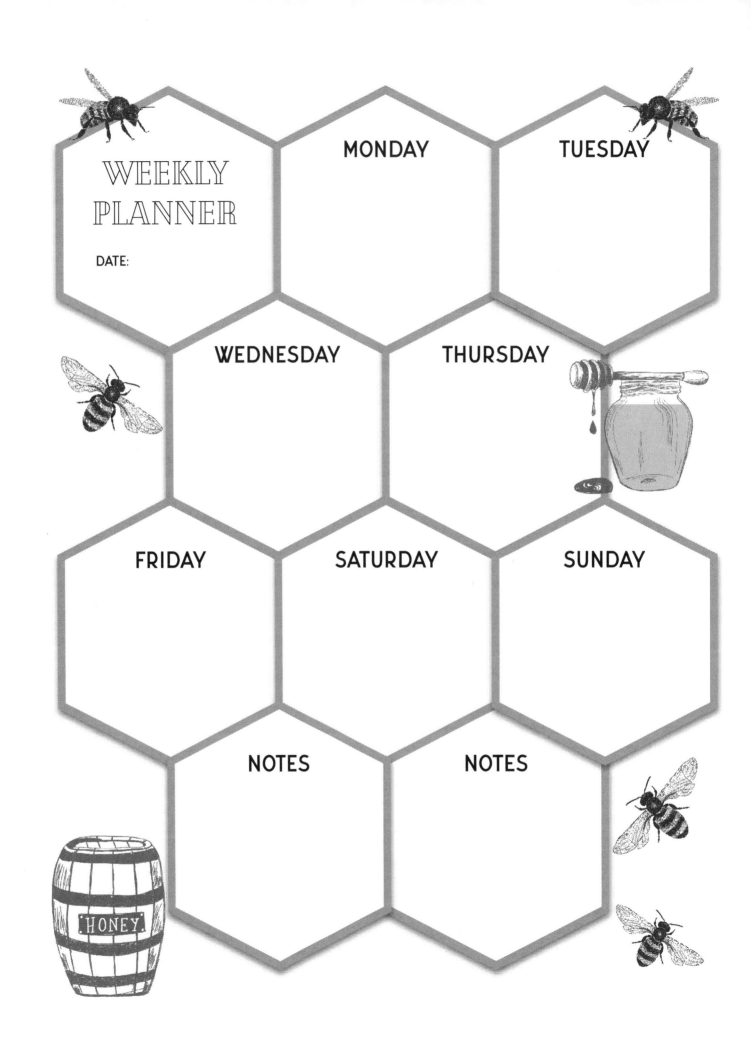

WEEKLY PLANNER

DATE:

MONDAY

TUESDAY

WEDNESDAY

THURSDAY

FRIDAY

SATURDAY

SUNDAY

NOTES

NOTES

HONEY

CHORES

WEEK:

NAME:

MONDAY

- ○
- ○
- ○
- ○
- ○
- ○

TUESDAY

- ○
- ○
- ○
- ○
- ○
- ○

WEDNESDAY

- ○
- ○
- ○
- ○
- ○
- ○

THURSDAY

- ○
- ○
- ○
- ○
- ○
- ○

FRIDAY

- ○
- ○
- ○
- ○
- ○
- ○

SATURDAY

- ○
- ○
- ○
- ○
- ○
- ○

SUNDAY

- ○
- ○
- ○
- ○
- ○

NOTES

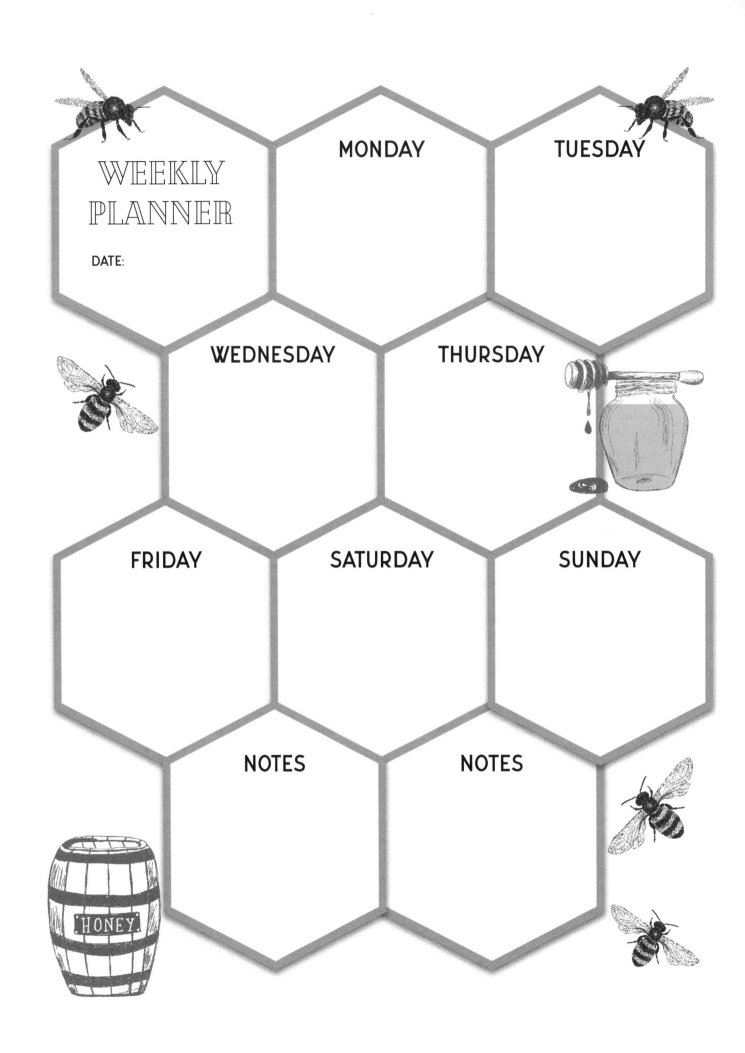

WEEKLY PLANNER

DATE:

MONDAY

TUESDAY

WEDNESDAY

THURSDAY

FRIDAY

SATURDAY

SUNDAY

NOTES

NOTES

HONEY

CHORES

WEEK:

NAME:

MONDAY

TUESDAY

WEDNESDAY

THURSDAY

FRIDAY

SATURDAY

SUNDAY

NOTES

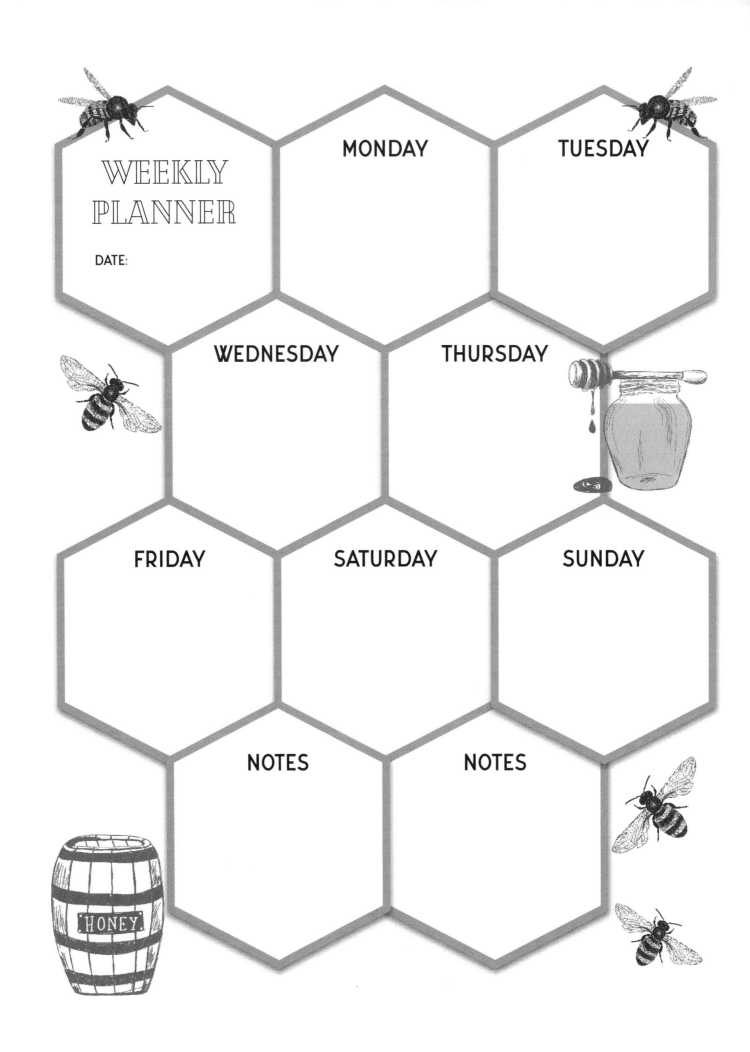

WEEKLY PLANNER

DATE:

MONDAY

TUESDAY

WEDNESDAY

THURSDAY

FRIDAY

SATURDAY

SUNDAY

NOTES

NOTES

CHORES

WEEK:

NAME:

MONDAY

- ○
- ○
- ○
- ○
- ○
- ○

TUESDAY

- ○
- ○
- ○
- ○
- ○
- ○

WEDNESDAY

- ○
- ○
- ○
- ○
- ○
- ○

THURSDAY

- ○
- ○
- ○
- ○
- ○
- ○

FRIDAY

- ○
- ○
- ○
- ○
- ○
- ○

SATURDAY

- ○
- ○
- ○
- ○
- ○
- ○

SUNDAY

- ○
- ○
- ○
- ○
- ○

NOTES

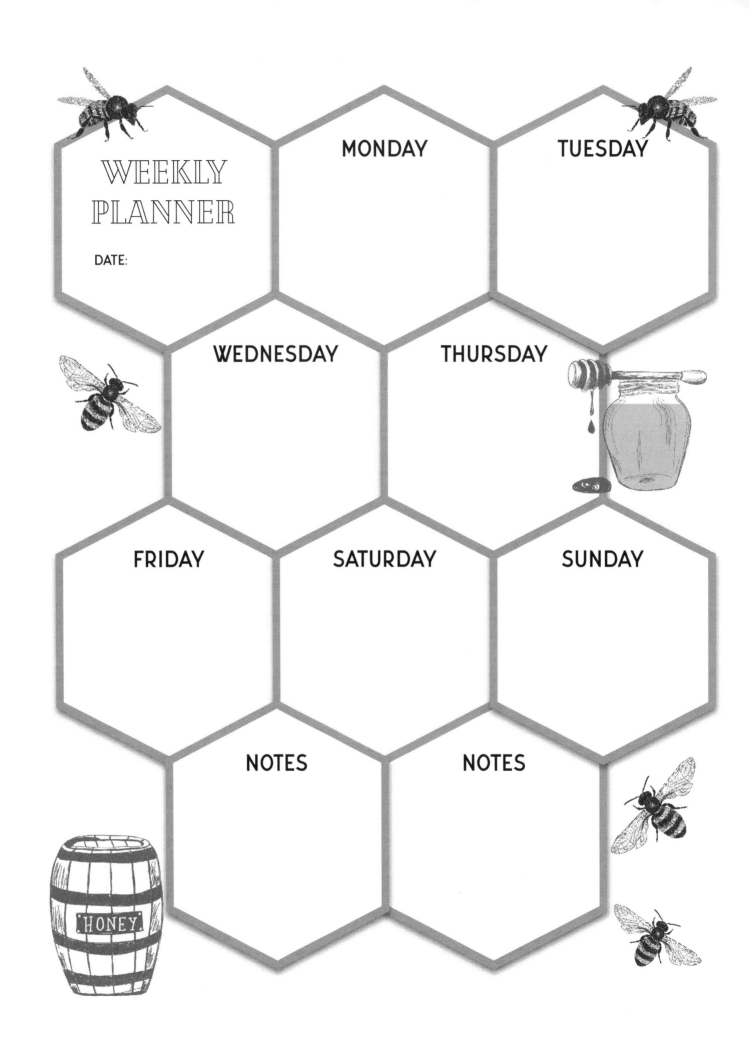

WEEKLY PLANNER

DATE:

MONDAY

TUESDAY

WEDNESDAY

THURSDAY

FRIDAY

SATURDAY

SUNDAY

NOTES

NOTES

HONEY

CHORES

WEEK:

NAME:

MONDAY
- ○
- ○
- ○
- ○
- ○
- ○

TUESDAY
- ○
- ○
- ○
- ○
- ○
- ○

WEDNESDAY
- ○
- ○
- ○
- ○
- ○
- ○

THURSDAY
- ○
- ○
- ○
- ○
- ○
- ○

FRIDAY
- ○
- ○
- ○
- ○
- ○
- ○

SATURDAY
- ○
- ○
- ○
- ○
- ○
- ○

SUNDAY
- ○
- ○
- ○
- ○
- ○

NOTES

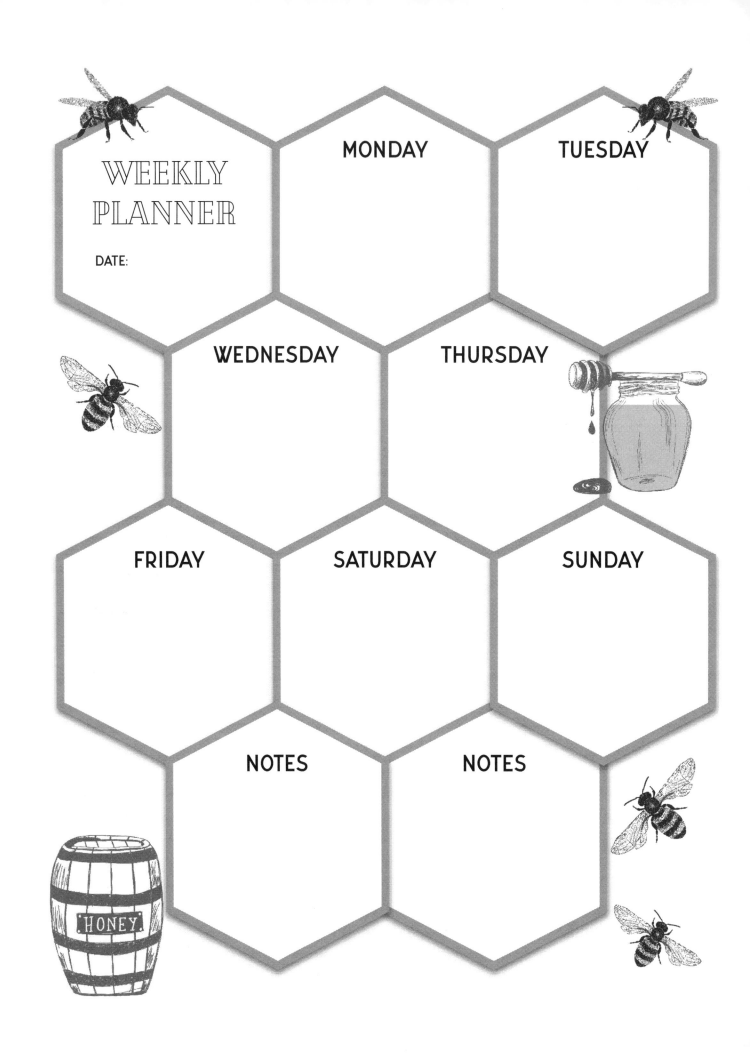

WEEKLY PLANNER

DATE:

MONDAY

TUESDAY

WEDNESDAY

THURSDAY

FRIDAY

SATURDAY

SUNDAY

NOTES

NOTES

CHORES

WEEK:

NAME:

MONDAY

	○
	○
	○
	○
	○
	○

TUESDAY

	○
	○
	○
	○
	○
	○

WEDNESDAY

	○
	○
	○
	○
	○
	○

THURSDAY

	○
	○
	○
	○
	○
	○

FRIDAY

	○
	○
	○
	○
	○
	○

SATURDAY

	○
	○
	○
	○
	○
	○

SUNDAY

	○
	○
	○
	○
	○

NOTES

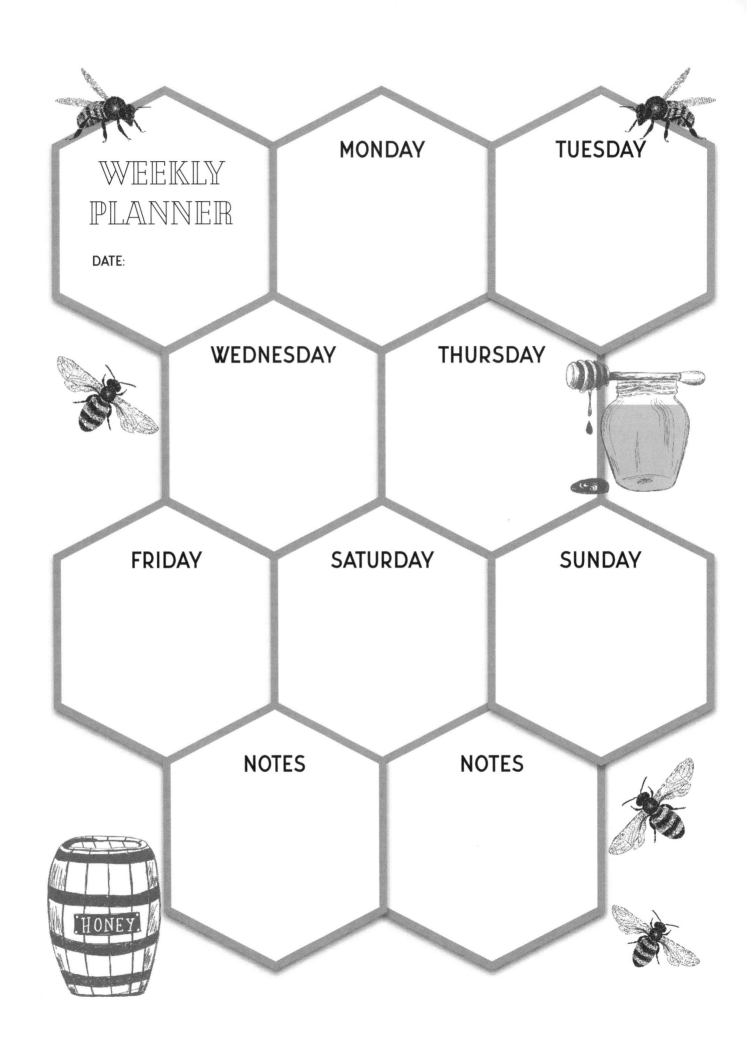

WEEKLY PLANNER

DATE:

MONDAY

TUESDAY

WEDNESDAY

THURSDAY

FRIDAY

SATURDAY

SUNDAY

NOTES

NOTES

HONEY

CHORES

WEEK:

NAME:

MONDAY
- ○
- ○
- ○
- ○
- ○
- ○

TUESDAY
- ○
- ○
- ○
- ○
- ○
- ○

WEDNESDAY
- ○
- ○
- ○
- ○
- ○
- ○

THURSDAY
- ○
- ○
- ○
- ○
- ○
- ○

FRIDAY
- ○
- ○
- ○
- ○
- ○
- ○

SATURDAY
- ○
- ○
- ○
- ○
- ○
- ○

SUNDAY
- ○
- ○
- ○
- ○
- ○

NOTES

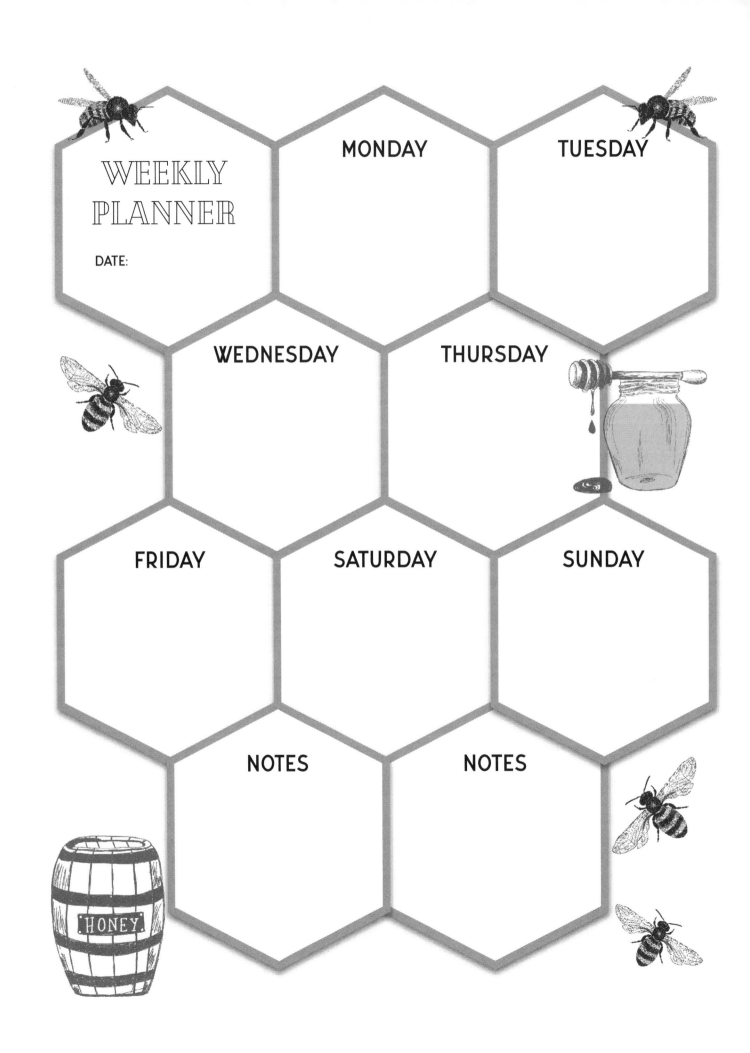

WEEKLY PLANNER

DATE:

MONDAY

TUESDAY

WEDNESDAY

THURSDAY

FRIDAY

SATURDAY

SUNDAY

NOTES

NOTES

CHORES

WEEK:

NAME:

MONDAY
- ○
- ○
- ○
- ○
- ○
- ○

TUESDAY
- ○
- ○
- ○
- ○
- ○
- ○

WEDNESDAY
- ○
- ○
- ○
- ○
- ○
- ○

THURSDAY
- ○
- ○
- ○
- ○
- ○
- ○

FRIDAY
- ○
- ○
- ○
- ○
- ○
- ○

SATURDAY
- ○
- ○
- ○
- ○
- ○
- ○

SUNDAY
- ○
- ○
- ○
- ○
- ○

NOTES

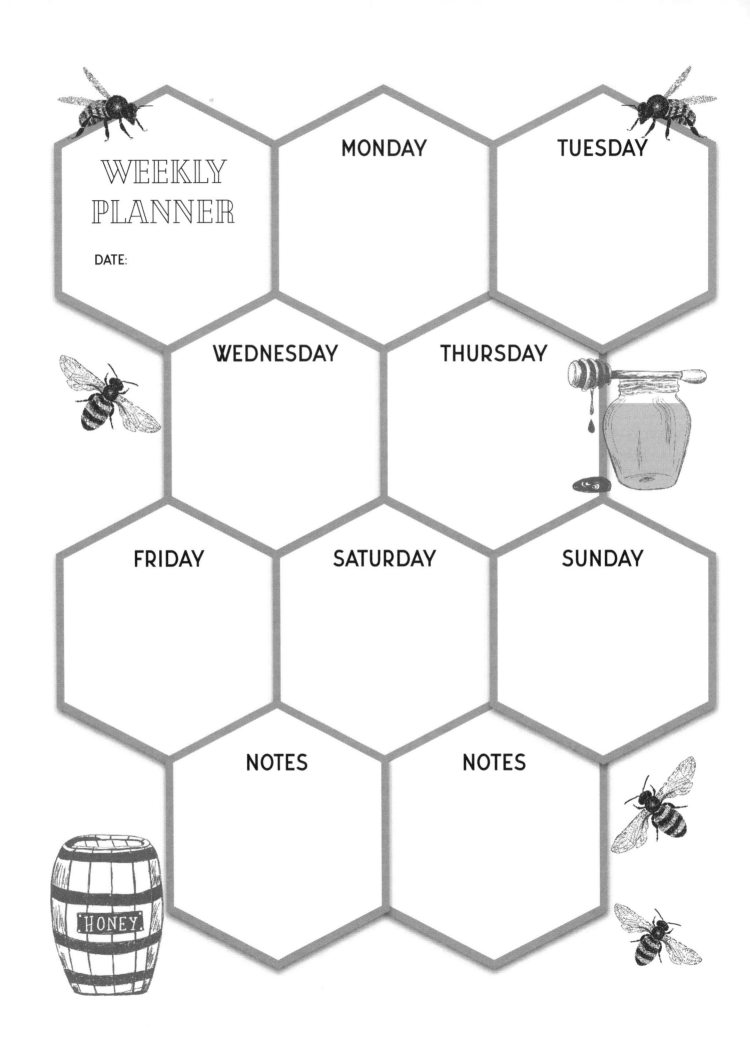

WEEKLY PLANNER

DATE:

MONDAY

TUESDAY

WEDNESDAY

THURSDAY

FRIDAY

SATURDAY

SUNDAY

NOTES

NOTES

HONEY

CHORES

WEEK:

NAME:

MONDAY

	○
	○
	○
	○
	○
	○

TUESDAY

	○
	○
	○
	○
	○
	○

WEDNESDAY

	○
	○
	○
	○
	○
	○

THURSDAY

	○
	○
	○
	○
	○
	○

FRIDAY

	○
	○
	○
	○
	○
	○

SATURDAY

	○
	○
	○
	○
	○
	○

SUNDAY

	○
	○
	○
	○
	○

NOTES

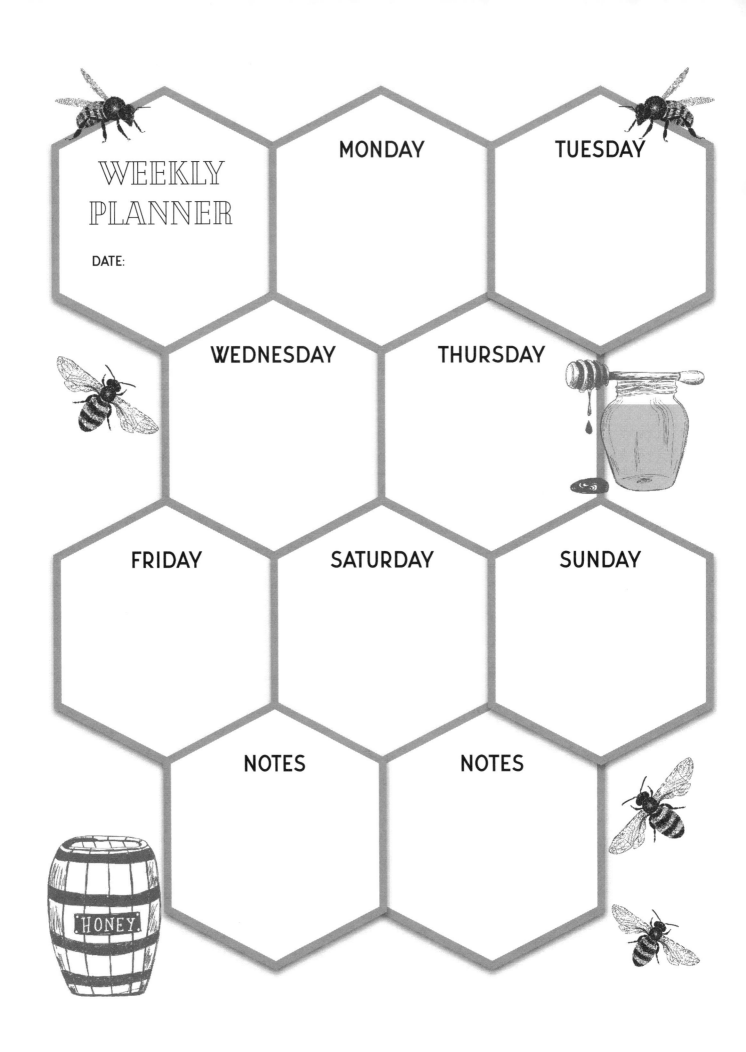

WEEKLY PLANNER

DATE:

MONDAY

TUESDAY

WEDNESDAY

THURSDAY

FRIDAY

SATURDAY

SUNDAY

NOTES

NOTES

CHORES

WEEK:

NAME:

MONDAY

	○
	○
	○
	○
	○
	○

TUESDAY

	○
	○
	○
	○
	○
	○

WEDNESDAY

	○
	○
	○
	○
	○
	○

THURSDAY

	○
	○
	○
	○
	○
	○

FRIDAY

	○
	○
	○
	○
	○
	○

SATURDAY

	○
	○
	○
	○
	○
	○

SUNDAY

	○
	○
	○
	○
	○

NOTES

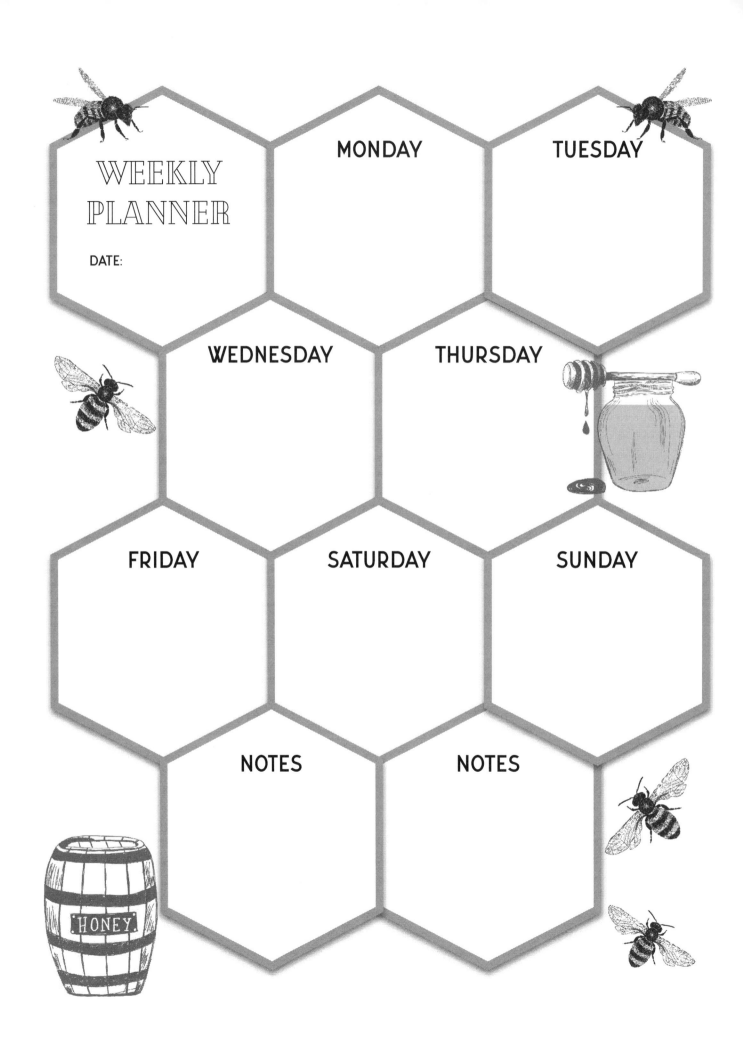

WEEKLY PLANNER

DATE:

MONDAY

TUESDAY

WEDNESDAY

THURSDAY

FRIDAY

SATURDAY

SUNDAY

NOTES

NOTES

CHORES

WEEK:

NAME:

MONDAY

	○
	○
	○
	○
	○
	○

TUESDAY

	○
	○
	○
	○
	○
	○

WEDNESDAY

	○
	○
	○
	○
	○
	○

THURSDAY

	○
	○
	○
	○
	○
	○

FRIDAY

	○
	○
	○
	○
	○
	○

SATURDAY

	○
	○
	○
	○
	○
	○

SUNDAY

	○
	○
	○
	○
	○

NOTES

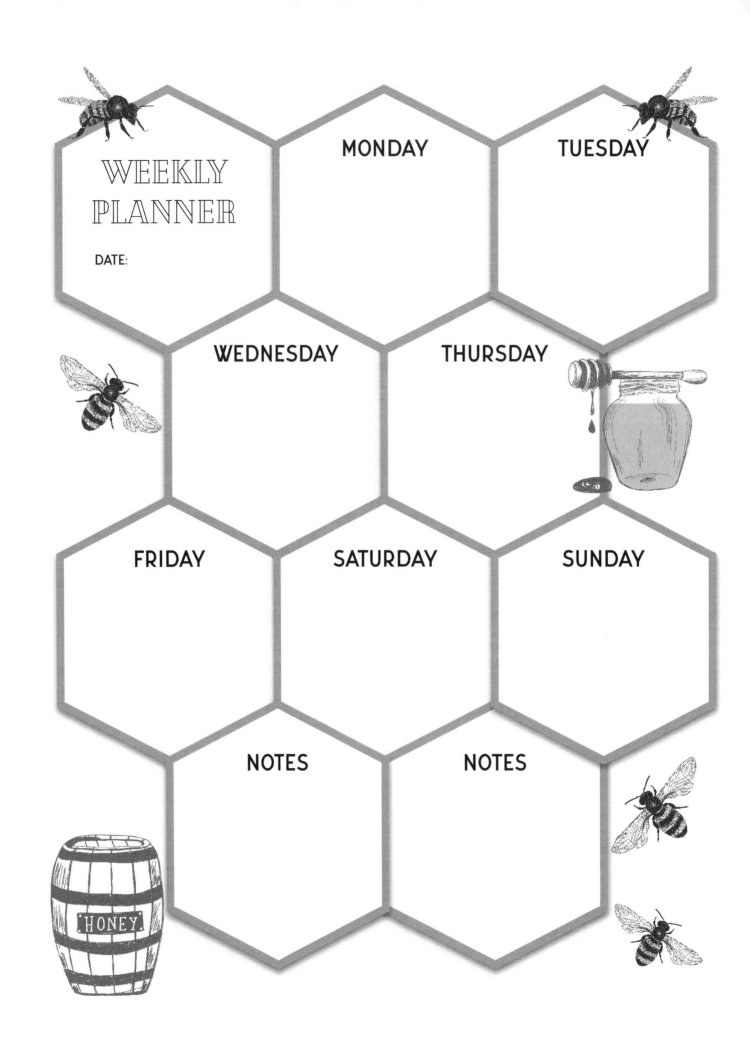

WEEKLY PLANNER

DATE:

MONDAY

TUESDAY

WEDNESDAY

THURSDAY

FRIDAY

SATURDAY

SUNDAY

NOTES

NOTES

HONEY

CHORES

MONDAY

	○
	○
	○
	○
	○
	○

TUESDAY

	○
	○
	○
	○
	○
	○

WEDNESDAY

	○
	○
	○
	○
	○
	○

THURSDAY

	○
	○
	○
	○
	○
	○

FRIDAY

	○
	○
	○
	○
	○
	○

SATURDAY

	○
	○
	○
	○
	○
	○

SUNDAY

	○
	○
	○
	○
	○

NOTES

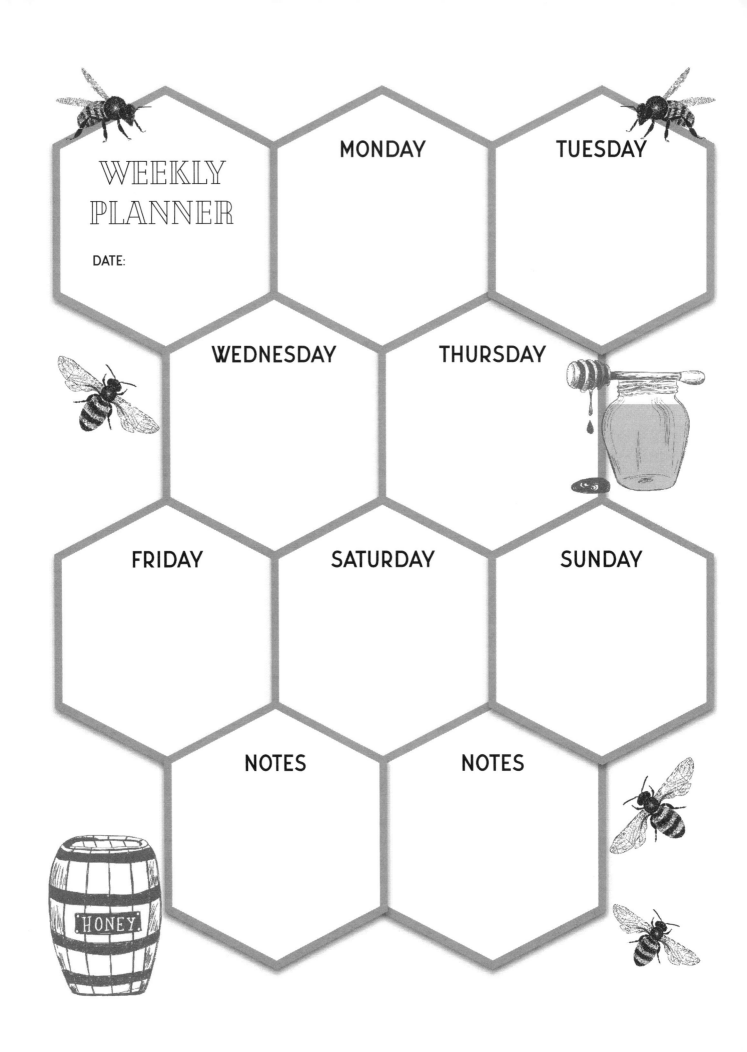

WEEKLY PLANNER

DATE:

MONDAY

TUESDAY

WEDNESDAY

THURSDAY

FRIDAY

SATURDAY

SUNDAY

NOTES

NOTES

HONEY

CHORES

WEEK:

NAME:

MONDAY

	○
	○
	○
	○
	○
	○

TUESDAY

	○
	○
	○
	○
	○
	○

WEDNESDAY

	○
	○
	○
	○
	○
	○

THURSDAY

	○
	○
	○
	○
	○
	○

FRIDAY

	○
	○
	○
	○
	○
	○

SATURDAY

	○
	○
	○
	○
	○
	○

SUNDAY

	○
	○
	○
	○
	○

NOTES

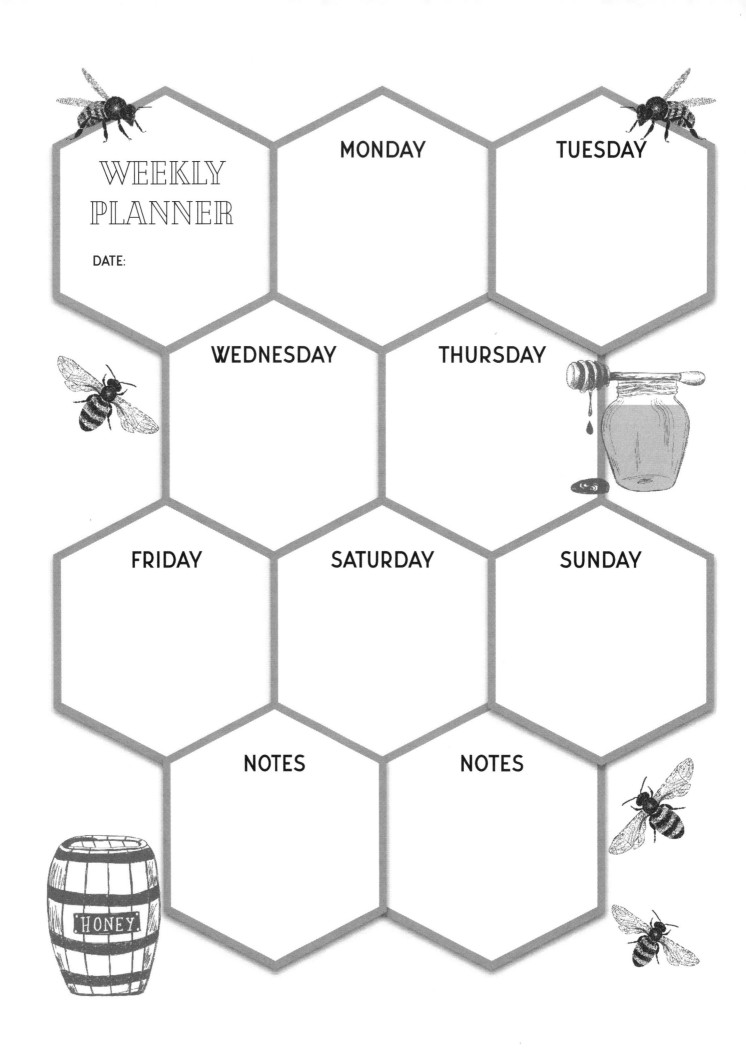

WEEKLY PLANNER

DATE:

MONDAY

TUESDAY

WEDNESDAY

THURSDAY

FRIDAY

SATURDAY

SUNDAY

NOTES

NOTES

HONEY

CHORES

WEEK:

NAME:

MONDAY

	○
	○
	○
	○
	○
	○

TUESDAY

	○
	○
	○
	○
	○
	○

WEDNESDAY

	○
	○
	○
	○
	○
	○

THURSDAY

	○
	○
	○
	○
	○
	○

FRIDAY

	○
	○
	○
	○
	○
	○

SATURDAY

	○
	○
	○
	○
	○
	○

SUNDAY

	○
	○
	○
	○
	○

NOTES

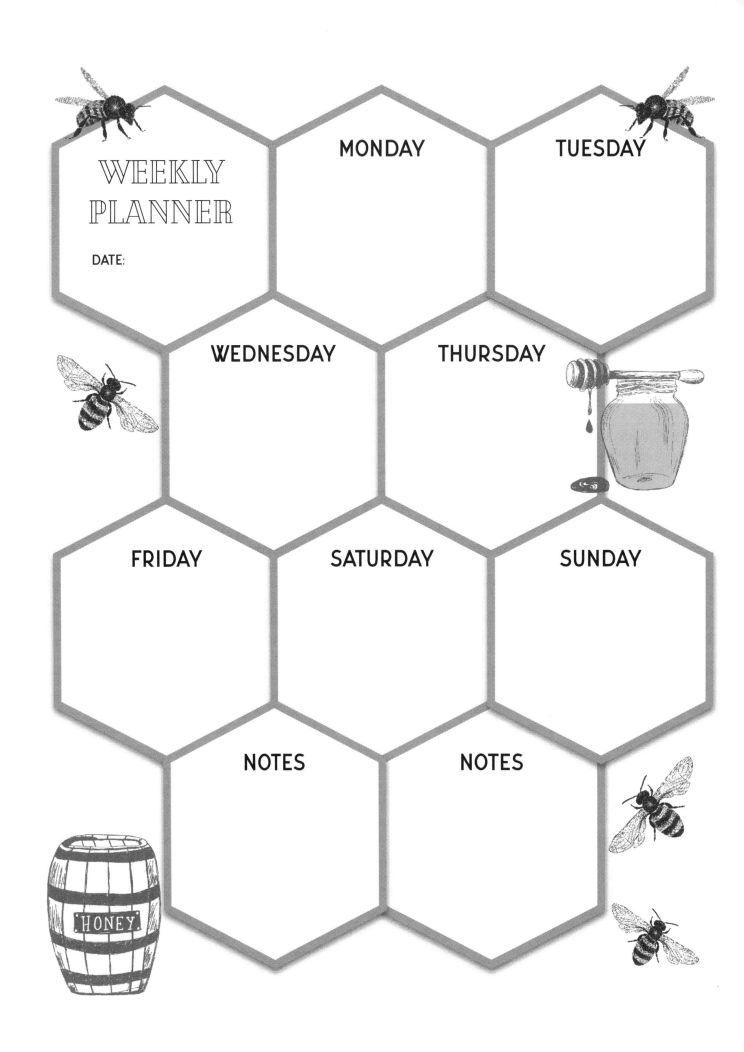

WEEKLY PLANNER

DATE:

MONDAY

TUESDAY

WEDNESDAY

THURSDAY

FRIDAY

SATURDAY

SUNDAY

NOTES

NOTES

HONEY

CHORES

WEEK:

NAME:

MONDAY

- ○
- ○
- ○
- ○
- ○
- ○

TUESDAY

- ○
- ○
- ○
- ○
- ○
- ○

WEDNESDAY

- ○
- ○
- ○
- ○
- ○
- ○

THURSDAY

- ○
- ○
- ○
- ○
- ○
- ○

FRIDAY

- ○
- ○
- ○
- ○
- ○
- ○

SATURDAY

- ○
- ○
- ○
- ○
- ○
- ○

SUNDAY

- ○
- ○
- ○
- ○
- ○

NOTES

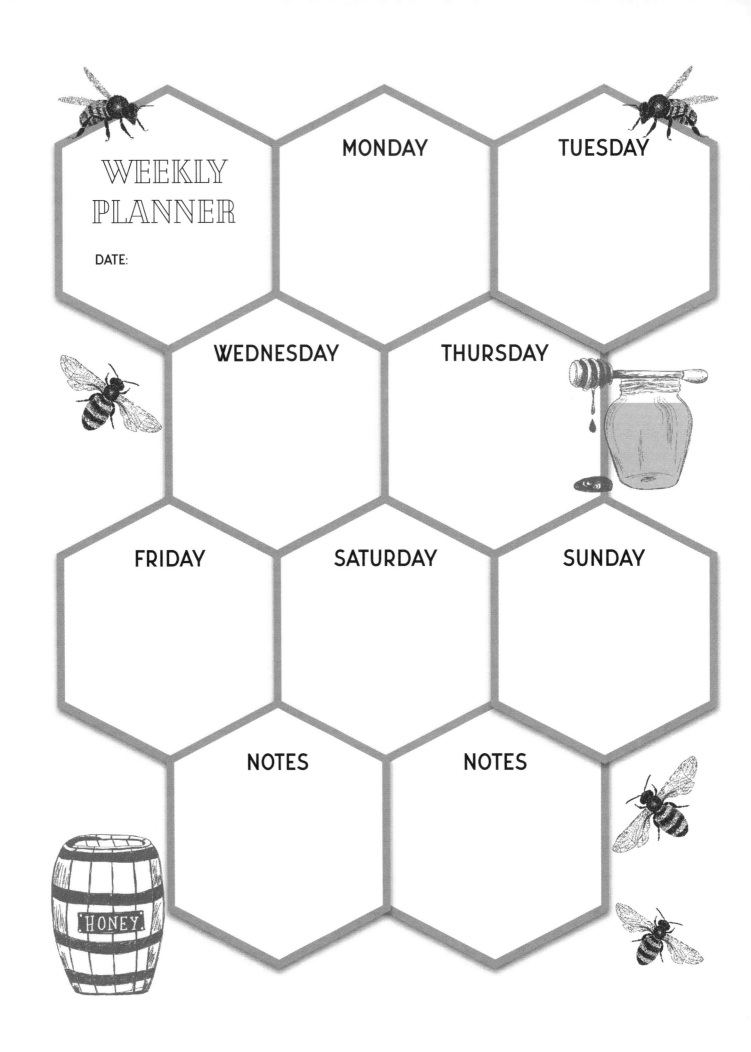

WEEKLY PLANNER

DATE:

MONDAY

TUESDAY

WEDNESDAY

THURSDAY

FRIDAY

SATURDAY

SUNDAY

NOTES

NOTES

HONEY

CHORES

WEEK:

NAME:

MONDAY
- ○
- ○
- ○
- ○
- ○
- ○

TUESDAY
- ○
- ○
- ○
- ○
- ○
- ○

WEDNESDAY
- ○
- ○
- ○
- ○
- ○
- ○

THURSDAY
- ○
- ○
- ○
- ○
- ○
- ○

FRIDAY
- ○
- ○
- ○
- ○
- ○
- ○

SATURDAY
- ○
- ○
- ○
- ○
- ○
- ○

SUNDAY
- ○
- ○
- ○
- ○
- ○

NOTES

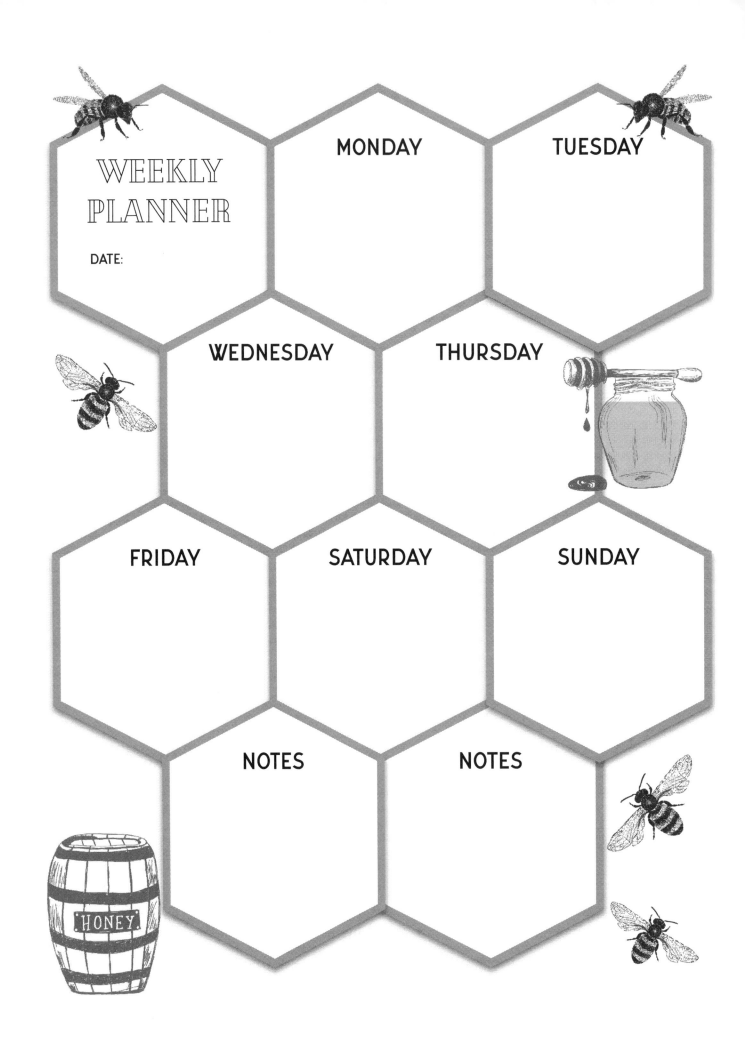

WEEKLY PLANNER

DATE:

MONDAY

TUESDAY

WEDNESDAY

THURSDAY

FRIDAY

SATURDAY

SUNDAY

NOTES

NOTES

CHORES

WEEK:

NAME:

MONDAY
	○
	○
	○
	○
	○
	○

TUESDAY
	○
	○
	○
	○
	○
	○

WEDNESDAY
	○
	○
	○
	○
	○
	○

THURSDAY
	○
	○
	○
	○
	○
	○

FRIDAY
	○
	○
	○
	○
	○
	○

SATURDAY
	○
	○
	○
	○
	○
	○

SUNDAY
	○
	○
	○
	○
	○

NOTES

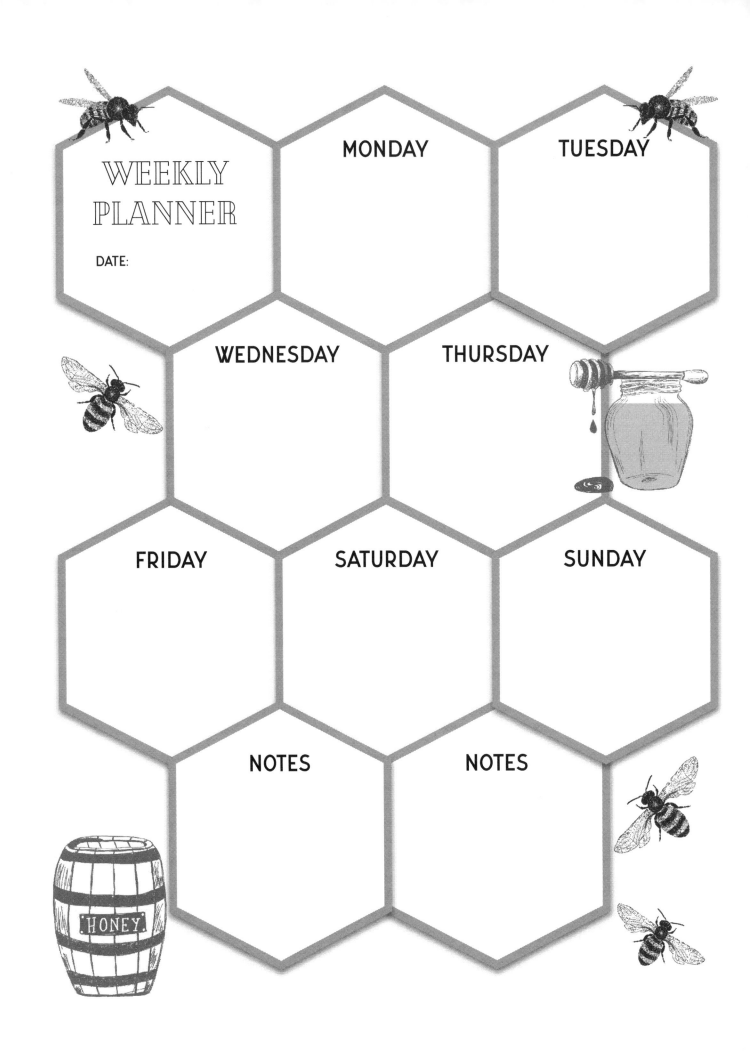

WEEKLY
PLANNER

DATE:

MONDAY

TUESDAY

WEDNESDAY

THURSDAY

FRIDAY

SATURDAY

SUNDAY

NOTES

NOTES

HONEY

CHORES

MONDAY

- ○
- ○
- ○
- ○
- ○
- ○

TUESDAY

- ○
- ○
- ○
- ○
- ○
- ○

WEDNESDAY

- ○
- ○
- ○
- ○
- ○
- ○

THURSDAY

- ○
- ○
- ○
- ○
- ○
- ○

FRIDAY

- ○
- ○
- ○
- ○
- ○
- ○

SATURDAY

- ○
- ○
- ○
- ○
- ○
- ○

SUNDAY

- ○
- ○
- ○
- ○
- ○

NOTES

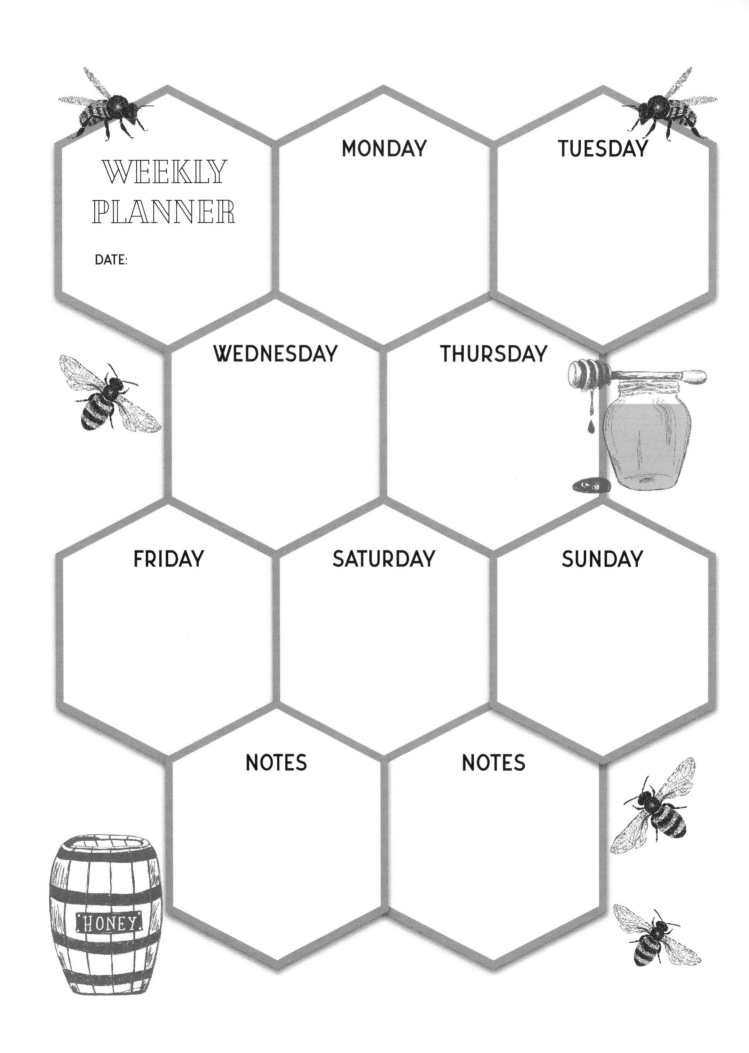

WEEKLY PLANNER

DATE:

MONDAY

TUESDAY

WEDNESDAY

THURSDAY

FRIDAY

SATURDAY

SUNDAY

NOTES

NOTES

HONEY

CHORES

WEEK:

NAME:

MONDAY

- ○
- ○
- ○
- ○
- ○
- ○

TUESDAY

- ○
- ○
- ○
- ○
- ○
- ○

WEDNESDAY

- ○
- ○
- ○
- ○
- ○
- ○

THURSDAY

- ○
- ○
- ○
- ○
- ○
- ○

FRIDAY

- ○
- ○
- ○
- ○
- ○
- ○

SATURDAY

- ○
- ○
- ○
- ○
- ○
- ○

SUNDAY

- ○
- ○
- ○
- ○
- ○

NOTES

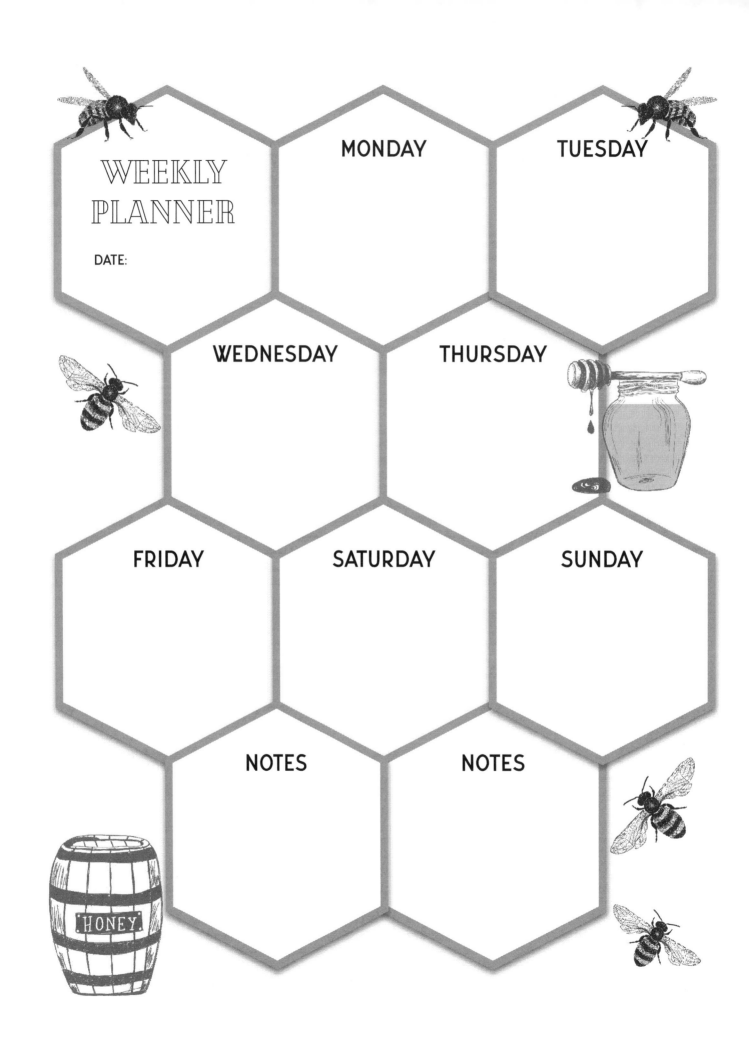

WEEKLY PLANNER

DATE:

MONDAY

TUESDAY

WEDNESDAY

THURSDAY

FRIDAY

SATURDAY

SUNDAY

NOTES

NOTES

HONEY.

CHORES

WEEK:

NAME:

MONDAY
- ○
- ○
- ○
- ○
- ○
- ○

TUESDAY
- ○
- ○
- ○
- ○
- ○
- ○

WEDNESDAY
- ○
- ○
- ○
- ○
- ○
- ○

THURSDAY
- ○
- ○
- ○
- ○
- ○
- ○

FRIDAY
- ○
- ○
- ○
- ○
- ○
- ○

SATURDAY
- ○
- ○
- ○
- ○
- ○
- ○

SUNDAY
- ○
- ○
- ○
- ○
- ○

NOTES

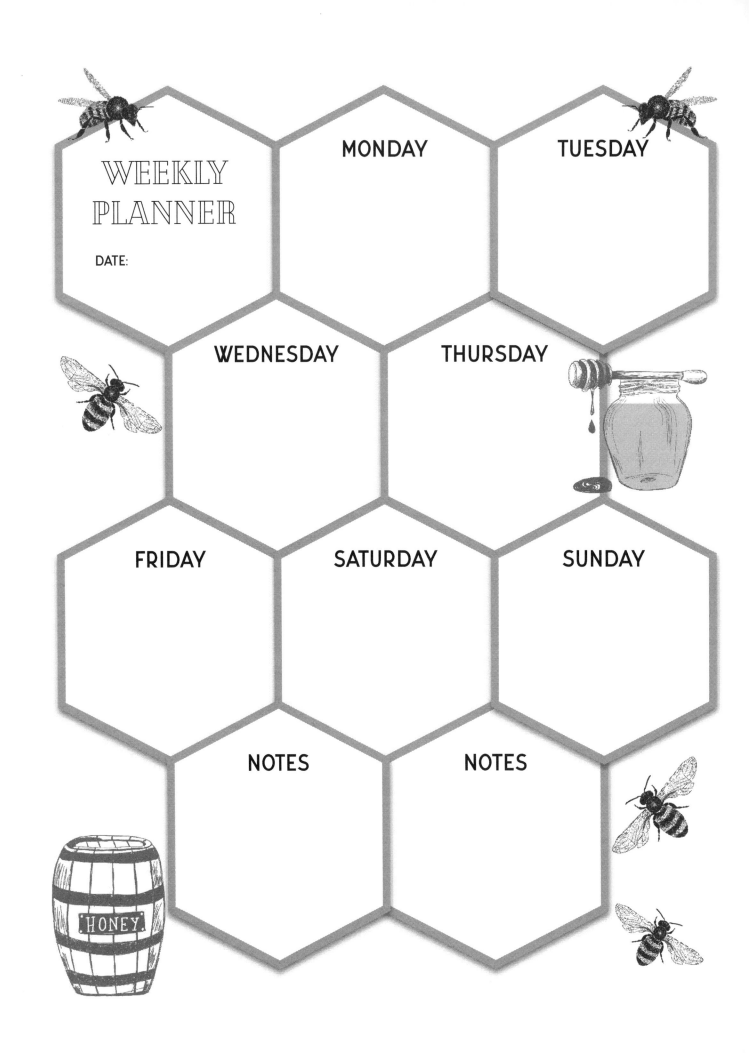

WEEKLY PLANNER

DATE:

MONDAY

TUESDAY

WEDNESDAY

THURSDAY

FRIDAY

SATURDAY

SUNDAY

NOTES

NOTES

HONEY

CHORES

WEEK:

NAME:

MONDAY
- ○
- ○
- ○
- ○
- ○
- ○

TUESDAY
- ○
- ○
- ○
- ○
- ○
- ○

WEDNESDAY
- ○
- ○
- ○
- ○
- ○
- ○

THURSDAY
- ○
- ○
- ○
- ○
- ○
- ○

FRIDAY
- ○
- ○
- ○
- ○
- ○
- ○

SATURDAY
- ○
- ○
- ○
- ○
- ○
- ○

SUNDAY
- ○
- ○
- ○
- ○
- ○

NOTES

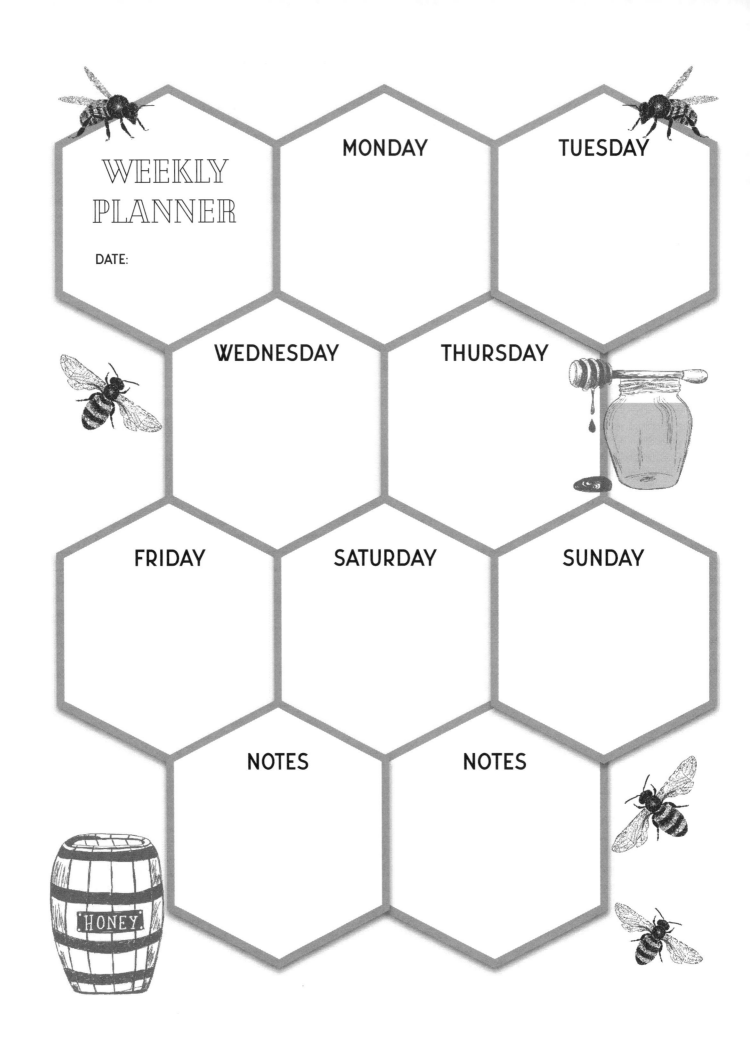

WEEKLY PLANNER

DATE:

MONDAY

TUESDAY

WEDNESDAY

THURSDAY

FRIDAY

SATURDAY

SUNDAY

NOTES

NOTES

HONEY

CHORES

WEEK:

NAME:

MONDAY

- ○
- ○
- ○
- ○
- ○
- ○

TUESDAY

- ○
- ○
- ○
- ○
- ○
- ○

WEDNESDAY

- ○
- ○
- ○
- ○
- ○
- ○

THURSDAY

- ○
- ○
- ○
- ○
- ○
- ○

FRIDAY

- ○
- ○
- ○
- ○
- ○
- ○

SATURDAY

- ○
- ○
- ○
- ○
- ○

SUNDAY

- ○
- ○
- ○
- ○
- ○

NOTES

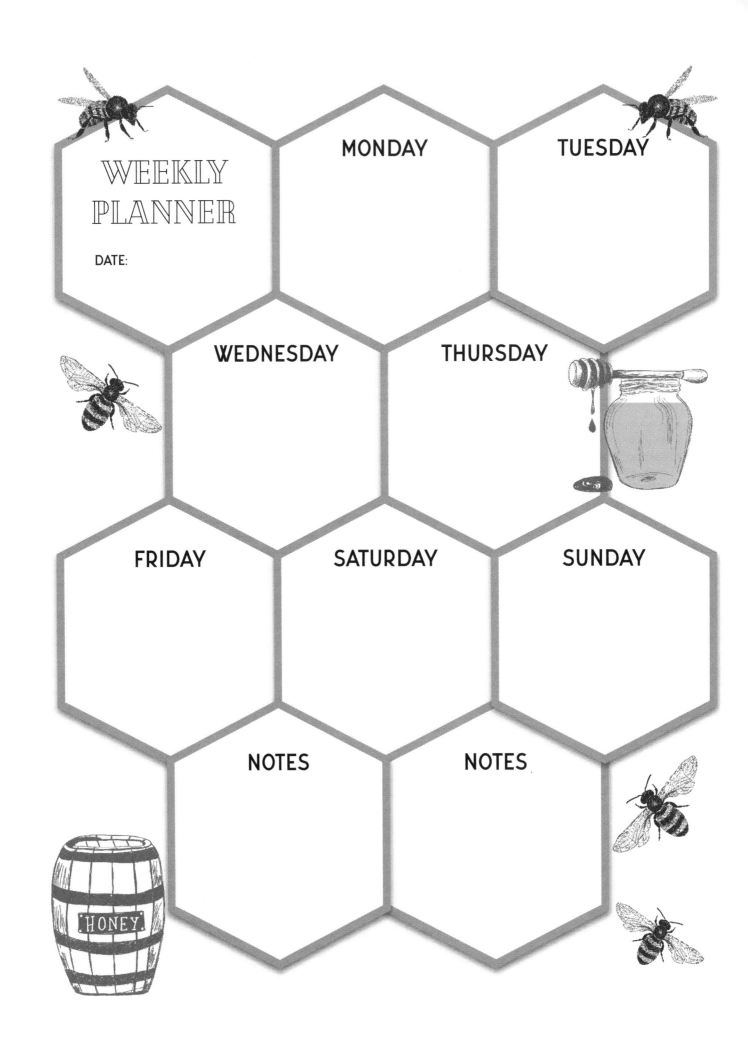

WEEKLY PLANNER

DATE:

MONDAY

TUESDAY

WEDNESDAY

THURSDAY

FRIDAY

SATURDAY

SUNDAY

NOTES

NOTES

CHORES

WEEK:

NAME:

MONDAY
- ○
- ○
- ○
- ○
- ○
- ○

TUESDAY
- ○
- ○
- ○
- ○
- ○
- ○

WEDNESDAY
- ○
- ○
- ○
- ○
- ○
- ○

THURSDAY
- ○
- ○
- ○
- ○
- ○
- ○

FRIDAY
- ○
- ○
- ○
- ○
- ○
- ○

SATURDAY
- ○
- ○
- ○
- ○
- ○
- ○

SUNDAY
- ○
- ○
- ○
- ○

NOTES

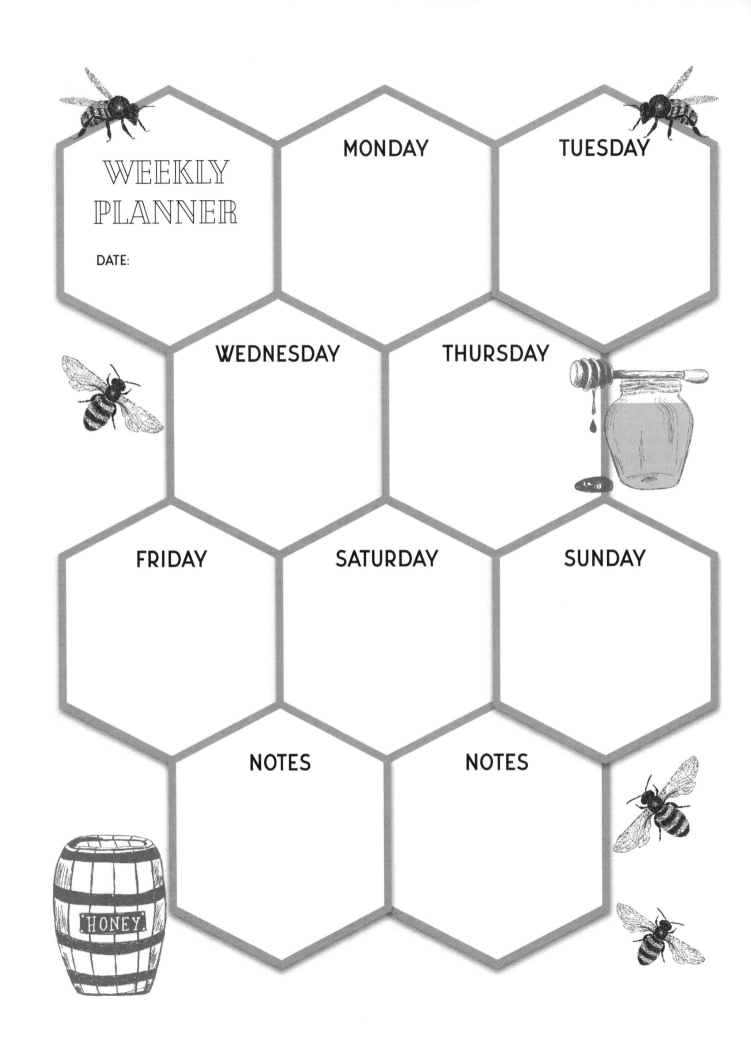

WEEKLY PLANNER

DATE:

MONDAY

TUESDAY

WEDNESDAY

THURSDAY

FRIDAY

SATURDAY

SUNDAY

NOTES

NOTES

HONEY

CHORES

WEEK:

NAME:

MONDAY
- ○
- ○
- ○
- ○
- ○
- ○

TUESDAY
- ○
- ○
- ○
- ○
- ○
- ○

WEDNESDAY
- ○
- ○
- ○
- ○
- ○
- ○

THURSDAY
- ○
- ○
- ○
- ○
- ○
- ○

FRIDAY
- ○
- ○
- ○
- ○
- ○
- ○

SATURDAY
- ○
- ○
- ○
- ○
- ○
- ○

SUNDAY
- ○
- ○
- ○
- ○
- ○

NOTES

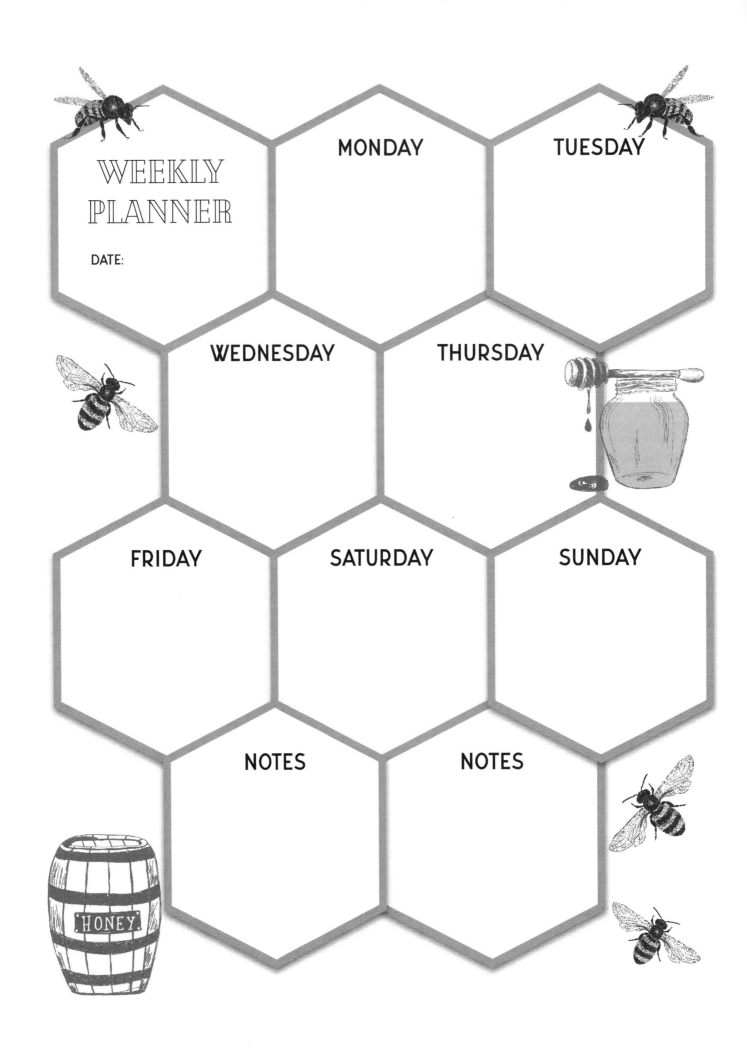

WEEKLY PLANNER

DATE:

MONDAY

TUESDAY

WEDNESDAY

THURSDAY

FRIDAY

SATURDAY

SUNDAY

NOTES

NOTES

HONEY

CHORES

WEEK:

NAME:

MONDAY	
	○
	○
	○
	○
	○
	○

TUESDAY	
	○
	○
	○
	○
	○
	○

WEDNESDAY	
	○
	○
	○
	○
	○
	○

THURSDAY	
	○
	○
	○
	○
	○
	○

FRIDAY	
	○
	○
	○
	○
	○
	○

SATURDAY	
	○
	○
	○
	○
	○
	○

SUNDAY	
	○
	○
	○
	○
	○

NOTES

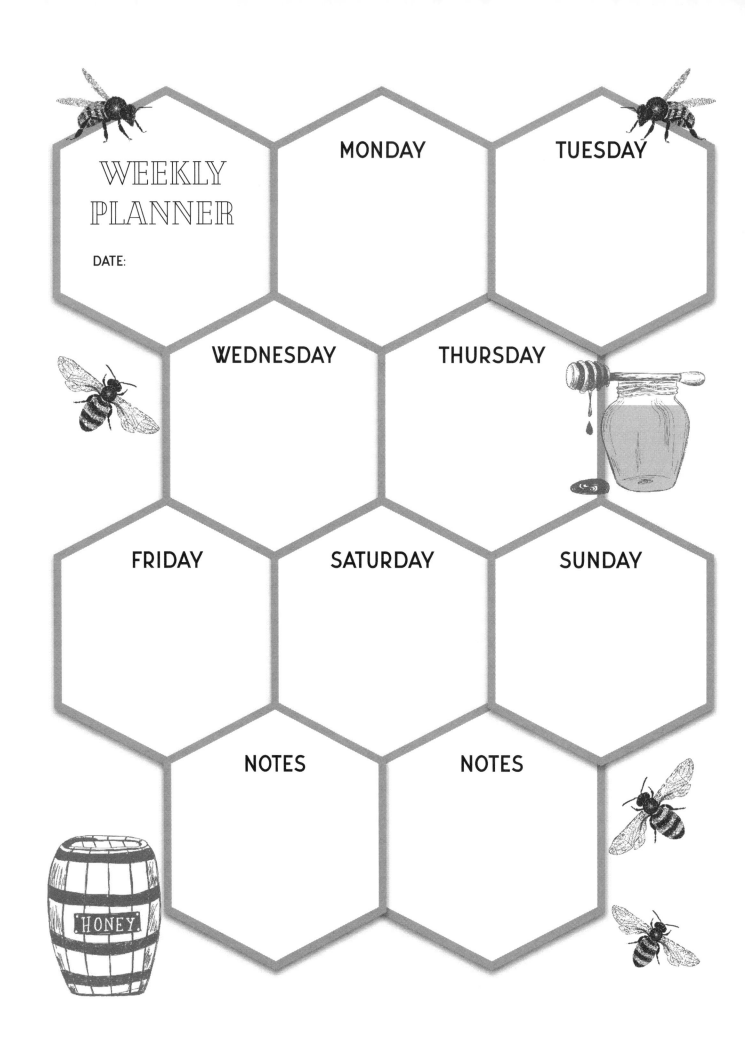

WEEKLY PLANNER

DATE:

MONDAY

TUESDAY

WEDNESDAY

THURSDAY

FRIDAY

SATURDAY

SUNDAY

NOTES

NOTES

HONEY

CHORES

WEEK:

NAME:

MONDAY
- ○
- ○
- ○
- ○
- ○
- ○

TUESDAY
- ○
- ○
- ○
- ○
- ○
- ○

WEDNESDAY
- ○
- ○
- ○
- ○
- ○
- ○

THURSDAY
- ○
- ○
- ○
- ○
- ○
- ○

FRIDAY
- ○
- ○
- ○
- ○
- ○
- ○

SATURDAY
- ○
- ○
- ○
- ○
- ○
- ○

SUNDAY
- ○
- ○
- ○
- ○
- ○

NOTES

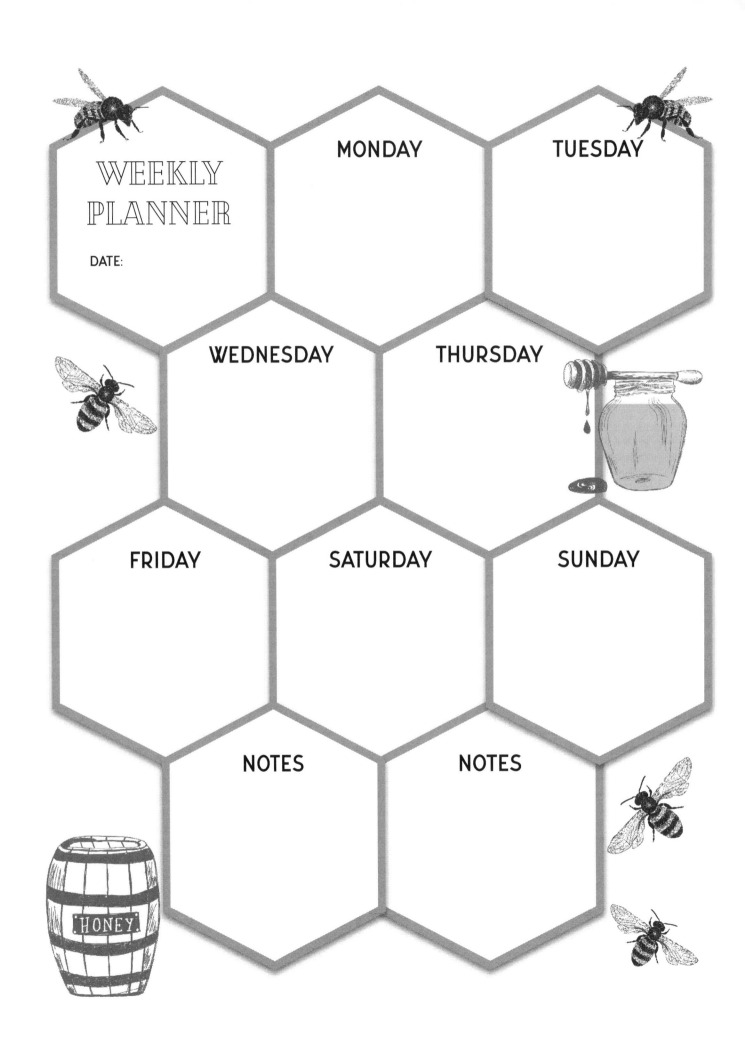

WEEKLY PLANNER

DATE:

MONDAY

TUESDAY

WEDNESDAY

THURSDAY

FRIDAY

SATURDAY

SUNDAY

NOTES

NOTES

HONEY.

CHORES

WEEK:

NAME:

MONDAY

	○
	○
	○
	○
	○
	○

TUESDAY

	○
	○
	○
	○
	○
	○

WEDNESDAY

	○
	○
	○
	○
	○
	○

THURSDAY

	○
	○
	○
	○
	○
	○

FRIDAY

	○
	○
	○
	○
	○
	○

SATURDAY

	○
	○
	○
	○
	○
	○

SUNDAY

	○
	○
	○
	○
	○

NOTES

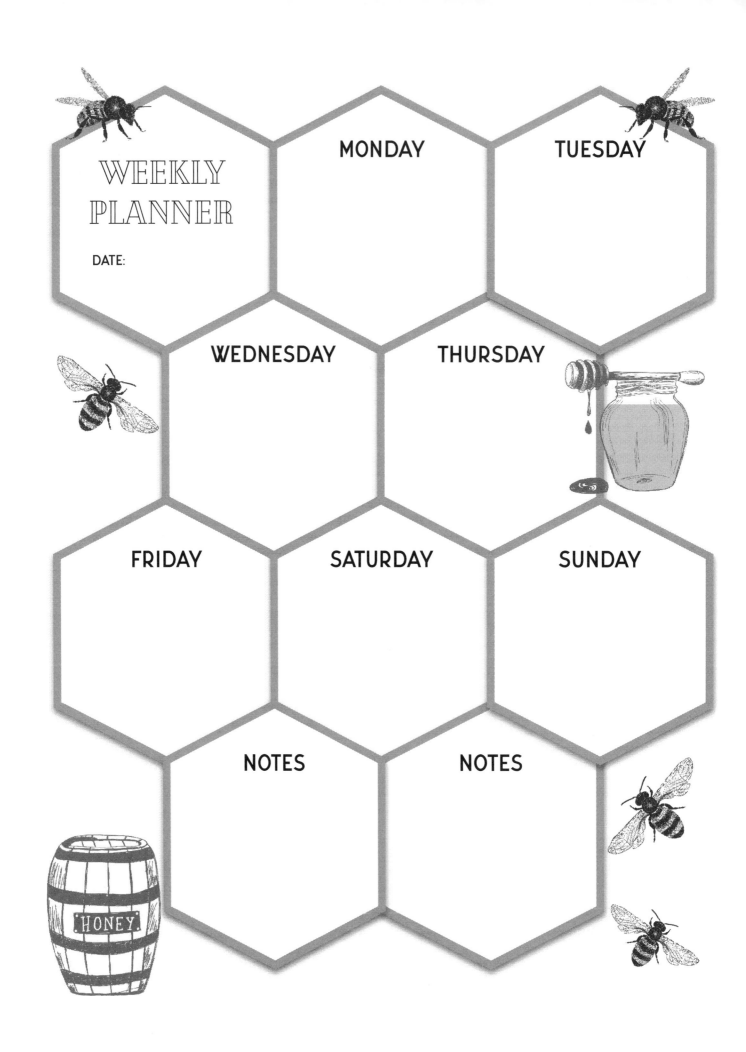

WEEKLY
PLANNER

DATE:

MONDAY

TUESDAY

WEDNESDAY

THURSDAY

FRIDAY

SATURDAY

SUNDAY

NOTES

NOTES

HONEY

CHORES

WEEK:

NAME:

MONDAY
	○
	○
	○
	○
	○
	○

TUESDAY
	○
	○
	○
	○
	○
	○

WEDNESDAY
	○
	○
	○
	○
	○
	○

THURSDAY
	○
	○
	○
	○
	○
	○

FRIDAY
	○
	○
	○
	○
	○
	○

SATURDAY
	○
	○
	○
	○
	○
	○

SUNDAY
	○
	○
	○
	○
	○

NOTES

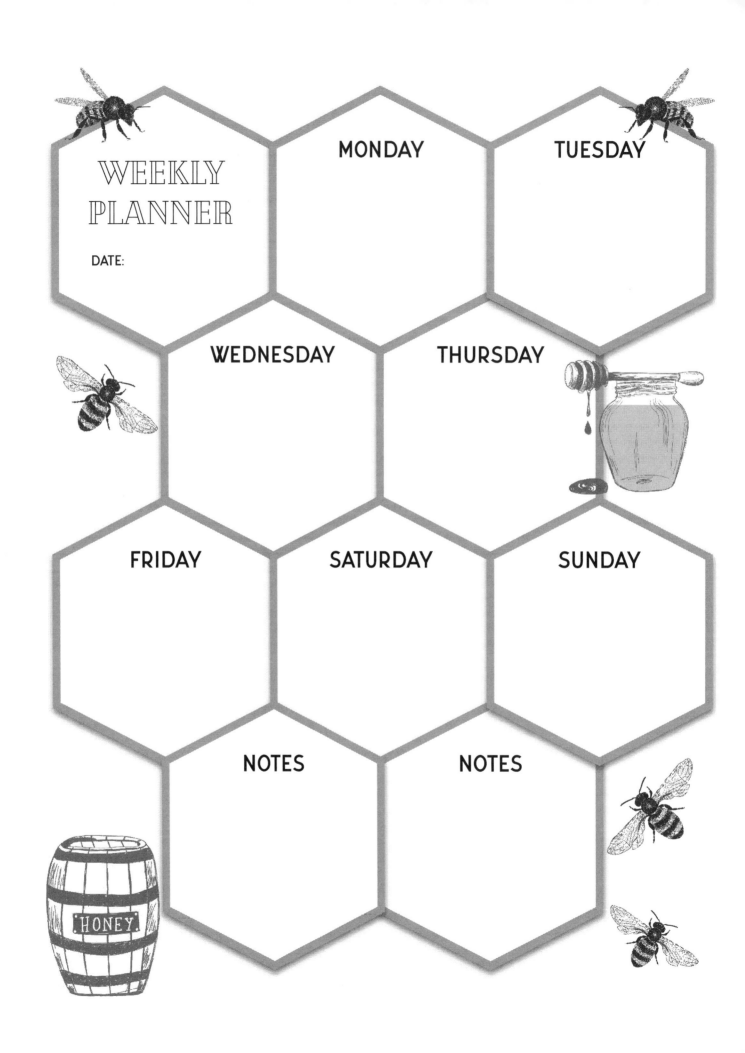

WEEKLY PLANNER

DATE:

MONDAY

TUESDAY

WEDNESDAY

THURSDAY

FRIDAY

SATURDAY

SUNDAY

NOTES

NOTES

HONEY

CHORES

WEEK:

NAME:

MONDAY
- ○
- ○
- ○
- ○
- ○
- ○

TUESDAY
- ○
- ○
- ○
- ○
- ○
- ○

WEDNESDAY
- ○
- ○
- ○
- ○
- ○
- ○

THURSDAY
- ○
- ○
- ○
- ○
- ○
- ○

FRIDAY
- ○
- ○
- ○
- ○
- ○
- ○

SATURDAY
- ○
- ○
- ○
- ○
- ○
- ○

SUNDAY
- ○
- ○
- ○
- ○
- ○

NOTES

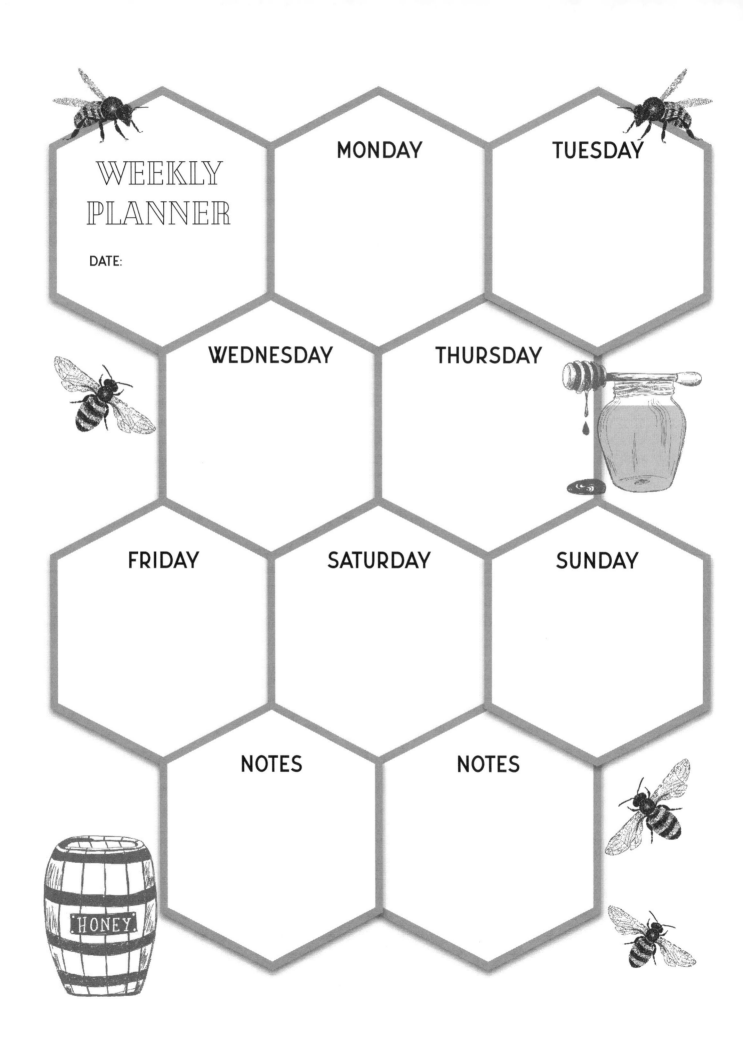

WEEKLY PLANNER

DATE:

MONDAY

TUESDAY

WEDNESDAY

THURSDAY

FRIDAY

SATURDAY

SUNDAY

NOTES

NOTES

HONEY.

CHORES

WEEK:

NAME:

MONDAY
- ○
- ○
- ○
- ○
- ○
- ○

TUESDAY
- ○
- ○
- ○
- ○
- ○
- ○

WEDNESDAY
- ○
- ○
- ○
- ○
- ○
- ○

THURSDAY
- ○
- ○
- ○
- ○
- ○
- ○

FRIDAY
- ○
- ○
- ○
- ○
- ○
- ○

SATURDAY
- ○
- ○
- ○
- ○
- ○
- ○

SUNDAY
- ○
- ○
- ○
- ○
- ○

NOTES

HOMESTEAD
FINANCES

MONTHLY INCOME

DATE	RECEIVED FROM	DETAILS	QTY	UNIT PRICE		AMOUNT	
				TOTAL			

MONTHLY EXPENSES

DATE	PAID TO	DETAILS	QTY	UNIT PRICE	AMOUNT
				TOTAL	

MONTHLY INCOME

DATE	RECEIVED FROM	DETAILS	QTY	UNIT PRICE	AMOUNT
				TOTAL	

MONTHLY EXPENSES

DATE	PAID TO	DETAILS	QTY	UNIT PRICE		AMOUNT	
				TOTAL			

MONTHLY INCOME

DATE	RECEIVED FROM	DETAILS	QTY	UNIT PRICE	AMOUNT	
				TOTAL		

MONTHLY EXPENSES

DATE	PAID TO	DETAILS	QTY	UNIT PRICE	AMOUNT
				TOTAL	

MONTHLY INCOME

DATE	RECEIVED FROM	DETAILS	QTY	UNIT PRICE	AMOUNT	
					TOTAL	

MONTHLY EXPENSES

DATE	PAID TO	DETAILS	QTY	UNIT PRICE		AMOUNT	
				TOTAL			

MONTHLY INCOME

DATE	RECEIVED FROM	DETAILS	QTY	UNIT PRICE	AMOUNT
				TOTAL	

MONTHLY EXPENSES

DATE	PAID TO	DETAILS	QTY	UNIT PRICE	AMOUNT	
				TOTAL		

MONTHLY INCOME

DATE	RECEIVED FROM	DETAILS	QTY	UNIT PRICE		AMOUNT	
					TOTAL		

MONTHLY EXPENSES

DATE	PAID TO	DETAILS	QTY	UNIT PRICE	AMOUNT
			TOTAL		

MONTHLY INCOME

DATE	RECEIVED FROM	DETAILS	QTY	UNIT PRICE	AMOUNT	
					TOTAL	

MONTHLY EXPENSES

DATE	PAID TO	DETAILS	QTY	UNIT PRICE		AMOUNT	
					TOTAL		

MONTHLY INCOME

DATE	RECEIVED FROM	DETAILS	QTY	UNIT PRICE		AMOUNT	
				TOTAL			

MONTHLY EXPENSES

DATE	PAID TO	DETAILS	QTY	UNIT PRICE		AMOUNT	
					TOTAL		

MONTHLY INCOME

DATE	RECEIVED FROM	DETAILS	QTY	UNIT PRICE		AMOUNT	
				TOTAL			

MONTHLY EXPENSES

DATE	PAID TO	DETAILS	QTY	UNIT PRICE	AMOUNT
				TOTAL	

MONTHLY INCOME

DATE	RECEIVED FROM	DETAILS	QTY	UNIT PRICE		AMOUNT	
					TOTAL		

MONTHLY EXPENSES

DATE	PAID TO	DETAILS	QTY	UNIT PRICE		AMOUNT	
					TOTAL		

MONTHLY INCOME

DATE	RECEIVED FROM	DETAILS	QTY	UNIT PRICE		AMOUNT	
					TOTAL		

MONTHLY EXPENSES

DATE	PAID TO	DETAILS	QTY	UNIT PRICE		AMOUNT	
					TOTAL		

MONTHLY INCOME

DATE	RECEIVED FROM	DETAILS	QTY	UNIT PRICE	AMOUNT	
				TOTAL		

MONTHLY EXPENSES

DATE	PAID TO	DETAILS	QTY	UNIT PRICE		AMOUNT	
				TOTAL			

GARDEN
PLANNER

GARDEN LAYOUT PLANNER

AREA / SEASON / MONTH _____

KEY

_____

_____

_____

_____

MONTHLY GARDEN PLANNER

PLANT	JANUARY				FEBRUARY				MARCH			
	1	2	3	4	1	2	3	4	1	2	3	4

NOTES

_____

_____

_____

_____

_____

_____

MONTHLY GARDEN PLANNER

PLANT	APRIL				MAY				JUNE			
	1	2	3	4	1	2	3	4	1	2	3	4

NOTES

_____

_____

_____

_____

_____

_____

MONTHLY GARDEN PLANNER

PLANT	JULY				AUGUST				SEPTEMBER			
	1	2	3	4	1	2	3	4	1	2	3	4

NOTES

_____

_____

_____

_____

_____

_____

MONTHLY GARDEN PLANNER

PLANT	OCTOBER				NOVEMBER				DECEMBER			
	1	2	3	4	1	2	3	4	1	2	3	4

NOTES

SEED PLANTING LOG

| PLANT | DATES | | | NOTES |
	PLANTED	GERMINATED	TRANSPLANTED	

SEED PLANTING LOG

PLANT	DATES			NOTES
	PLANTED	GERMINATED	TRANSPLANTED	

SEED PLANTING LOG

PLANT	DATES			NOTES
	PLANTED	GERMINATED	TRANSPLANTED	

SEED HARVEST LOG

PLANT	YIELD	DATES			NOTES
		PLANTED	HARVESTED	EXPIRY	

FLOWER TRACKER

NAME			DESCRIPTION	
EXPOSURE	**HEIGHT**	**DATE PLANTED**	**HARVEST DATE**	**YIELD**

BEST PLANTED NEAR	
CARE INSTRUCTIONS	

PESTS AND DISEASES	SYMPTOMS	CURES

HARVEST NOTES

NAME			DESCRIPTION	
EXPOSURE	**HEIGHT**	**DATE PLANTED**	**HARVEST DATE**	**YIELD**

BEST PLANTED NEAR	
CARE INSTRUCTIONS	

PESTS AND DISEASES	SYMPTOMS	CURES

HARVEST NOTES

FLOWER TRACKER

NAME	DESCRIPTION			
EXPOSURE	**HEIGHT**	**DATE PLANTED**	**HARVEST DATE**	**YIELD**

BEST PLANTED NEAR	
CARE INSTRUCTIONS	

PESTS AND DISEASES	SYMPTOMS	CURES

HARVEST NOTES

NAME	DESCRIPTION			
EXPOSURE	**HEIGHT**	**DATE PLANTED**	**HARVEST DATE**	**YIELD**

BEST PLANTED NEAR	
CARE INSTRUCTIONS	

PESTS AND DISEASES	SYMPTOMS	CURES

HARVEST NOTES

FLOWER TRACKER

NAME	DESCRIPTION			
EXPOSURE	HEIGHT	DATE PLANTED	HARVEST DATE	YIELD

BEST PLANTED NEAR	
CARE INSTRUCTIONS	

PESTS AND DISEASES	SYMPTOMS	CURES

HARVEST NOTES

NAME	DESCRIPTION			
EXPOSURE	HEIGHT	DATE PLANTED	HARVEST DATE	YIELD

BEST PLANTED NEAR	
CARE INSTRUCTIONS	

PESTS AND DISEASES	SYMPTOMS	CURES

HARVEST NOTES

FLOWER TRACKER

NAME	DESCRIPTION			
EXPOSURE	HEIGHT	DATE PLANTED	HARVEST DATE	YIELD

BEST PLANTED NEAR	
CARE INSTRUCTIONS	

PESTS AND DISEASES	SYMPTOMS	CURES

HARVEST NOTES

NAME	DESCRIPTION			
EXPOSURE	HEIGHT	DATE PLANTED	HARVEST DATE	YIELD

BEST PLANTED NEAR	
CARE INSTRUCTIONS	

PESTS AND DISEASES	SYMPTOMS	CURES

HARVEST NOTES

FLOWER HARVEST LOG

FLOWER	DATES		YIELD	NOTES
	PLANTED	HARVESTED		

HERB TRACKER

NAME	DESCRIPTION		

EXPOSURE	HEIGHT	DATE PLANTED	HARVEST DATE	YIELD

BEST PLANTED NEAR	
CARE INSTRUCTIONS	

PESTS AND DISEASES	SYMPTOMS	CURES

HARVEST NOTES

NAME	DESCRIPTION		

EXPOSURE	HEIGHT	DATE PLANTED	HARVEST DATE	YIELD

BEST PLANTED NEAR	
CARE INSTRUCTIONS	

PESTS AND DISEASES	SYMPTOMS	CURES

HARVEST NOTES

HERB TRACKER

NAME	DESCRIPTION

EXPOSURE	HEIGHT	DATE PLANTED	HARVEST DATE	YIELD

BEST PLANTED NEAR	
CARE INSTRUCTIONS	

PESTS AND DISEASES	SYMPTOMS	CURES

HARVEST NOTES

NAME	DESCRIPTION

EXPOSURE	HEIGHT	DATE PLANTED	HARVEST DATE	YIELD

BEST PLANTED NEAR	
CARE INSTRUCTIONS	

PESTS AND DISEASES	SYMPTOMS	CURES

HARVEST NOTES

HERB TRACKER

NAME		DESCRIPTION		
EXPOSURE	HEIGHT	DATE PLANTED	HARVEST DATE	YIELD

BEST PLANTED NEAR	
CARE INSTRUCTIONS	

PESTS AND DISEASES	SYMPTOMS	CURES

HARVEST NOTES

NAME		DESCRIPTION		
EXPOSURE	HEIGHT	DATE PLANTED	HARVEST DATE	YIELD

BEST PLANTED NEAR	
CARE INSTRUCTIONS	

PESTS AND DISEASES	SYMPTOMS	CURES

HARVEST NOTES

HERB TRACKER

NAME	DESCRIPTION			
EXPOSURE	HEIGHT	DATE PLANTED	HARVEST DATE	YIELD

BEST PLANTED NEAR	
CARE INSTRUCTIONS	

PESTS AND DISEASES	SYMPTOMS	CURES

HARVEST NOTES

NAME	DESCRIPTION			
EXPOSURE	HEIGHT	DATE PLANTED	HARVEST DATE	YIELD

BEST PLANTED NEAR	
CARE INSTRUCTIONS	

PESTS AND DISEASES	SYMPTOMS	CURES

HARVEST NOTES

HERB HARVEST LOG

HERB	DATES		YIELD	NOTES
	PLANTED	HARVESTED		

FRUIT & VEGETABLE TRACKER

NAME			DESCRIPTION		
EXPOSURE	HEIGHT	DATE PLANTED	HARVEST DATE	YIELD

BEST PLANTED NEAR	
CARE INSTRUCTIONS	

PESTS AND DISEASES	SYMPTOMS	CURES

HARVEST NOTES

NAME			DESCRIPTION		
EXPOSURE	HEIGHT	DATE PLANTED	HARVEST DATE	YIELD

BEST PLANTED NEAR	
CARE INSTRUCTIONS	

PESTS AND DISEASES	SYMPTOMS	CURES

HARVEST NOTES

FRUIT & VEGETABLE TRACKER

NAME		DESCRIPTION		
EXPOSURE	HEIGHT	DATE PLANTED	HARVEST DATE	YIELD

BEST PLANTED NEAR	
CARE INSTRUCTIONS	

PESTS AND DISEASES	SYMPTOMS	CURES

HARVEST NOTES

NAME		DESCRIPTION		
EXPOSURE	HEIGHT	DATE PLANTED	HARVEST DATE	YIELD

BEST PLANTED NEAR	
CARE INSTRUCTIONS	

PESTS AND DISEASES	SYMPTOMS	CURES

HARVEST NOTES

FRUIT & VEGETABLE TRACKER

NAME	DESCRIPTION

EXPOSURE	HEIGHT	DATE PLANTED	HARVEST DATE	YIELD

BEST PLANTED NEAR	
CARE INSTRUCTIONS	

PESTS AND DISEASES	SYMPTOMS	CURES

HARVEST NOTES

NAME	DESCRIPTION

EXPOSURE	HEIGHT	DATE PLANTED	HARVEST DATE	YIELD

BEST PLANTED NEAR	
CARE INSTRUCTIONS	

PESTS AND DISEASES	SYMPTOMS	CURES

HARVEST NOTES

FRUIT & VEGETABLE TRACKER

NAME	DESCRIPTION

EXPOSURE	HEIGHT	DATE PLANTED	HARVEST DATE	YIELD

BEST PLANTED NEAR	
CARE INSTRUCTIONS	

PESTS AND DISEASES	SYMPTOMS	CURES

HARVEST NOTES

NAME	DESCRIPTION

EXPOSURE	HEIGHT	DATE PLANTED	HARVEST DATE	YIELD

BEST PLANTED NEAR	
CARE INSTRUCTIONS	

PESTS AND DISEASES	SYMPTOMS	CURES

HARVEST NOTES

FRUIT & VEGETABLE HARVEST LOG

FRUIT / VEGETABLE	DATES		YIELD	NOTES
	PLANTED	HARVESTED		

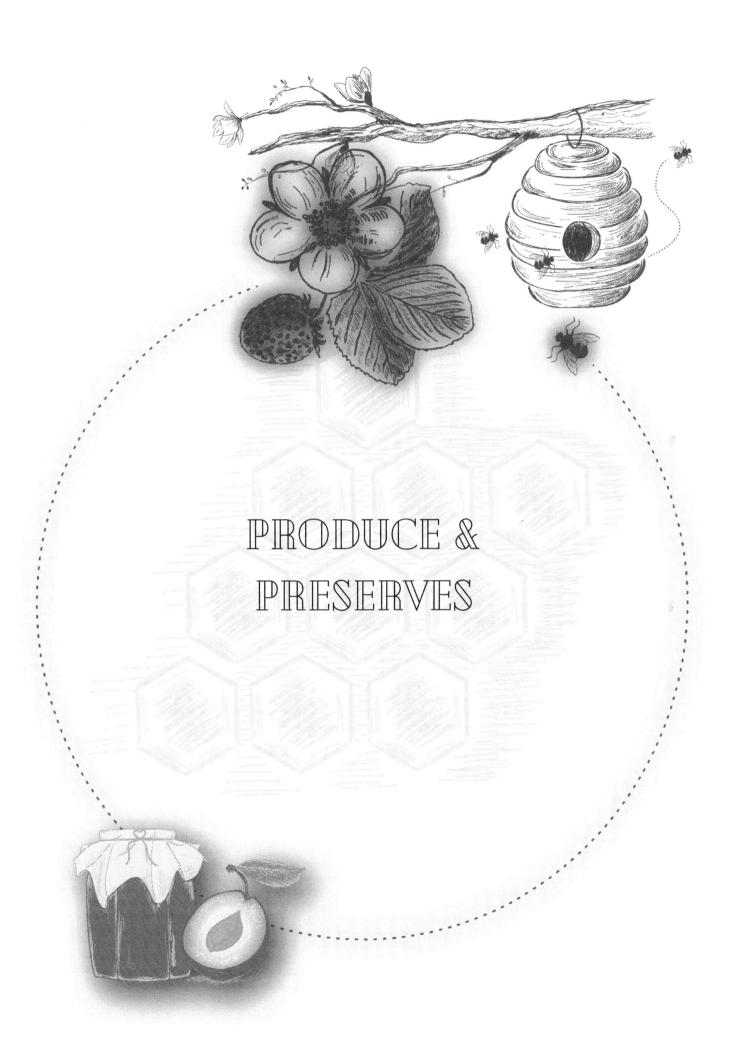

PRODUCE & PRESERVES

PRODUCE PRESERVATION

PRESERVATION TYPE		STANDING TIME	
		SHELF LIFE	
INGREDIENTS	ITEMS REQUIRED	METHOD	

PRESERVATION TYPE		STANDING TIME	
		SHELF LIFE	
INGREDIENTS	ITEMS REQUIRED	METHOD	

PRODUCE PRESERVATION

PRESERVATION TYPE		STANDING TIME	
		SHELF LIFE	
INGREDIENTS	ITEMS REQUIRED	METHOD	

PRESERVATION TYPE		STANDING TIME	
		SHELF LIFE	
INGREDIENTS	ITEMS REQUIRED	METHOD	

PRODUCE PRESERVATION

PRESERVATION TYPE		STANDING TIME	
		SHELF LIFE	
INGREDIENTS	ITEMS REQUIRED	METHOD	

PRESERVATION TYPE		STANDING TIME	
		SHELF LIFE	
INGREDIENTS	ITEMS REQUIRED	METHOD	

PRODUCE PRESERVATION

PRESERVATION TYPE		STANDING TIME	
		SHELF LIFE	
INGREDIENTS	ITEMS REQUIRED	METHOD	

PRESERVATION TYPE		STANDING TIME	
		SHELF LIFE	
INGREDIENTS	ITEMS REQUIRED	METHOD	

PRODUCE PRESERVATION

PRESERVATION TYPE		STANDING TIME	
		SHELF LIFE	
INGREDIENTS	ITEMS REQUIRED	METHOD	

PRESERVATION TYPE		STANDING TIME	
		SHELF LIFE	
INGREDIENTS	ITEMS REQUIRED	METHOD	

PRODUCE PRESERVATION

PRESERVATION TYPE		STANDING TIME	
		SHELF LIFE	
INGREDIENTS	ITEMS REQUIRED	METHOD	

PRESERVATION TYPE		STANDING TIME	
		SHELF LIFE	
INGREDIENTS	ITEMS REQUIRED	METHOD	

PRESERVES RECIPE

NAME	STANDING TIME	

INGREDIENTS	

METHOD

PRESERVES RECIPE

NAME	STANDING TIME	

INGREDIENTS	

METHOD

PRESERVES RECIPE

NAME	STANDING TIME	

INGREDIENTS

METHOD

PRESERVES RECIPE

NAME	STANDING TIME	

INGREDIENTS	

METHOD

PRESERVES RECIPE

NAME	STANDING TIME	

INGREDIENTS	

METHOD

PRESERVES RECIPE

NAME	STANDING TIME	

INGREDIENTS

METHOD

PRESERVES RECIPE

NAME	STANDING TIME	

INGREDIENTS	

METHOD

CHICKEN KEEPING
RECORDS

MONTHLY EGG PRODUCTION

MONTH							

	CHICKENS			EGGS			NOTES
	LAYING	MOLTING	TOTAL	TOTAL	BROKEN	REMAINING	
1							
2							
3							
4							
5							
6							
7							
8							
9							
10							
11							
12							
13							
14							
15							
16							
17							
18							
19							
20							
21							
22							
23							
24							
25							
26							
27							
28							
29							
30							
31							
TOTAL							

MONTHLY EGG PRODUCTION

MONTH							

	CHICKENS			EGGS			NOTES
	LAYING	MOLTING	TOTAL	TOTAL	BROKEN	REMAINING	
1							
2							
3							
4							
5							
6							
7							
8							
9							
10							
11							
12							
13							
14							
15							
16							
17							
18							
19							
20							
21							
22							
23							
24							
25							
26							
27							
28							
29							
30							
31							
TOTAL							

MONTHLY EGG PRODUCTION

MONTH							

	CHICKENS			EGGS			NOTES
	LAYING	MOLTING	TOTAL	TOTAL	BROKEN	REMAINING	
1							
2							
3							
4							
5							
6							
7							
8							
9							
10							
11							
12							
13							
14							
15							
16							
17							
18							
19							
20							
21							
22							
23							
24							
25							
26							
27							
28							
29							
30							
31							
TOTAL							

MONTHLY EGG PRODUCTION

MONTH							
	CHICKENS			EGGS			NOTES
	LAYING	MOLTING	TOTAL	TOTAL	BROKEN	REMAINING	
1							
2							
3							
4							
5							
6							
7							
8							
9							
10							
11							
12							
13							
14							
15							
16							
17							
18							
19							
20							
21							
22							
23							
24							
25							
26							
27							
28							
29							
30							
31							
TOTAL							

MONTHLY EGG PRODUCTION

| MONTH | | |

	CHICKENS			EGGS			NOTES
	LAYING	MOLTING	TOTAL	TOTAL	BROKEN	REMAINING	
1							
2							
3							
4							
5							
6							
7							
8							
9							
10							
11							
12							
13							
14							
15							
16							
17							
18							
19							
20							
21							
22							
23							
24							
25							
26							
27							
28							
29							
30							
31							
TOTAL							

MONTHLY EGG PRODUCTION

MONTH							

	CHICKENS			EGGS			NOTES
	LAYING	MOLTING	TOTAL	TOTAL	BROKEN	REMAINING	
1							
2							
3							
4							
5							
6							
7							
8							
9							
10							
11							
12							
13							
14							
15							
16							
17							
18							
19							
20							
21							
22							
23							
24							
25							
26							
27							
28							
29							
30							
31							
TOTAL							

MONTHLY EGG PRODUCTION

MONTH							
	CHICKENS			EGGS			NOTES
	LAYING	MOLTING	TOTAL	TOTAL	BROKEN	REMAINING	
1							
2							
3							
4							
5							
6							
7							
8							
9							
10							
11							
12							
13							
14							
15							
16							
17							
18							
19							
20							
21							
22							
23							
24							
25							
26							
27							
28							
29							
30							
31							
TOTAL							

MONTHLY EGG PRODUCTION

MONTH							

	CHICKENS			EGGS			NOTES
	LAYING	MOLTING	TOTAL	TOTAL	BROKEN	REMAINING	
1							
2							
3							
4							
5							
6							
7							
8							
9							
10							
11							
12							
13							
14							
15							
16							
17							
18							
19							
20							
21							
22							
23							
24							
25							
26							
27							
28							
29							
30							
31							
TOTAL							

MONTHLY EGG PRODUCTION

MONTH							
	CHICKENS			**EGGS**			**NOTES**
	LAYING	MOLTING	TOTAL	TOTAL	BROKEN	REMAINING	
1							
2							
3							
4							
5							
6							
7							
8							
9							
10							
11							
12							
13							
14							
15							
16							
17							
18							
19							
20							
21							
22							
23							
24							
25							
26							
27							
28							
29							
30							
31							
TOTAL							

MONTHLY EGG PRODUCTION

MONTH							
	CHICKENS			EGGS			NOTES
	LAYING	MOLTING	TOTAL	TOTAL	BROKEN	REMAINING	
1							
2							
3							
4							
5							
6							
7							
8							
9							
10							
11							
12							
13							
14							
15							
16							
17							
18							
19							
20							
21							
22							
23							
24							
25							
26							
27							
28							
29							
30							
31							
TOTAL							

MONTHLY EGG PRODUCTION

MONTH							

	CHICKENS			EGGS			NOTES
	LAYING	MOLTING	TOTAL	TOTAL	BROKEN	REMAINING	
1							
2							
3							
4							
5							
6							
7							
8							
9							
10							
11							
12							
13							
14							
15							
16							
17							
18							
19							
20							
21							
22							
23							
24							
25							
26							
27							
28							
29							
30							
31							
TOTAL							

MONTHLY EGG PRODUCTION

MONTH							

	CHICKENS			EGGS			NOTES
	LAYING	MOLTING	TOTAL	TOTAL	BROKEN	REMAINING	
1							
2							
3							
4							
5							
6							
7							
8							
9							
10							
11							
12							
13							
14							
15							
16							
17							
18							
19							
20							
21							
22							
23							
24							
25							
26							
27							
28							
29							
30							
31							
TOTAL							

ANNUAL EGG PRODUCTION

DATE	J	F	M	A	M	J	J	A	S	O	N	D
1												
2												
3												
4												
5												
6												
7												
8												
9												
10												
11												
12												
13												
14												
15												
16												
17												
18												
19												
20												
21												
22												
23												
24												
25												
26												
27												
28												
29												
30												
31												
TOTALS												

BEEKEEPING

BEEHIVE INSPECTION

Date		Weather		Temperature	

	HIVE #1	HIVE #2	HIVE #3	HIVE #4	HIVE #5	NOTES
HIVE SIZE						
QUEEN						
• MARKED						
• UNMARKED						
BROOD						
• EGGS						
• LARVAE						
• CAPPED						
QUEEN CELLS						
• SUPERCEDURE						
• SWARM						
FOOD						
• UNCAPPED HONEY						
• # CAPPED HONEY FRAMES						
• POLLEN						
PESTS						
• VARROA						
• WAX MOTHS						
TEMPERAMENT						
• CALM						
• AGGRESSIVE						
POPULATION						
• LOW						
• THRIVING						
• HIGH						
YIELD						

BEEHIVE INSPECTION

Date		Weather		Temperature	

	HIVE #1	HIVE #2	HIVE #3	HIVE #4	HIVE #5	NOTES
HIVE SIZE						
QUEEN						
• MARKED						
• UNMARKED						
BROOD						
• EGGS						
• LARVAE						
• CAPPED						
QUEEN CELLS						
• SUPERCEDURE						
• SWARM						
FOOD						
• UNCAPPED HONEY						
• # CAPPED HONEY FRAMES						
• POLLEN						
PESTS						
• VARROA						
• WAX MOTHS						
TEMPERAMENT						
• CALM						
• AGGRESSIVE						
POPULATION						
• LOW						
• THRIVING						
• HIGH						
YIELD						

BEEHIVE INSPECTION

Date		Weather		Temperature	

	HIVE #1	HIVE #2	HIVE #3	HIVE #4	HIVE #5	NOTES
HIVE SIZE						
QUEEN						
• MARKED						
• UNMARKED						
BROOD						
• EGGS						
• LARVAE						
• CAPPED						
QUEEN CELLS						
• SUPERCEDURE						
• SWARM						
FOOD						
• UNCAPPED HONEY						
• # CAPPED HONEY FRAMES						
• POLLEN						
PESTS						
• VARROA						
• WAX MOTHS						
TEMPERAMENT						
• CALM						
• AGGRESSIVE						
POPULATION						
• LOW						
• THRIVING						
• HIGH						
YIELD						

BEEHIVE INSPECTION

Date		Weather		Temperature	

	HIVE #1	HIVE #2	HIVE #3	HIVE #4	HIVE #5	NOTES
HIVE SIZE						
QUEEN						
• MARKED						
• UNMARKED						
BROOD						
• EGGS						
• LARVAE						
• CAPPED						
QUEEN CELLS						
• SUPERCEDURE						
• SWARM						
FOOD						
• UNCAPPED HONEY						
• # CAPPED HONEY FRAMES						
• POLLEN						
PESTS						
• VARROA						
• WAX MOTHS						
TEMPERAMENT						
• CALM						
• AGGRESSIVE						
POPULATION						
• LOW						
• THRIVING						
• HIGH						
YIELD						

BEEHIVE INSPECTION

Date		Weather		Temperature	

	HIVE #1	HIVE #2	HIVE #3	HIVE #4	HIVE #5	NOTES
HIVE SIZE						
QUEEN						
• MARKED						
• UNMARKED						
BROOD						
• EGGS						
• LARVAE						
• CAPPED						
QUEEN CELLS						
• SUPERCEDURE						
• SWARM						
FOOD						
• UNCAPPED HONEY						
• # CAPPED HONEY FRAMES						
• POLLEN						
PESTS						
• VARROA						
• WAX MOTHS						
TEMPERAMENT						
• CALM						
• AGGRESSIVE						
POPULATION						
• LOW						
• THRIVING						
• HIGH						
YIELD						

BEEHIVE INSPECTION

Date		Weather		Temperature	

	HIVE #1	HIVE #2	HIVE #3	HIVE #4	HIVE #5	NOTES
HIVE SIZE						
QUEEN						
• MARKED						
• UNMARKED						
BROOD						
• EGGS						
• LARVAE						
• CAPPED						
QUEEN CELLS						
• SUPERCEDURE						
• SWARM						
FOOD						
• UNCAPPED HONEY						
• # CAPPED HONEY FRAMES						
• POLLEN						
PESTS						
• VARROA						
• WAX MOTHS						
TEMPERAMENT						
• CALM						
• AGGRESSIVE						
POPULATION						
• LOW						
• THRIVING						
• HIGH						
YIELD						

BEEHIVE INSPECTION

Date		Weather		Temperature	

	HIVE #1	HIVE #2	HIVE #3	HIVE #4	HIVE #5	NOTES
HIVE SIZE						
QUEEN						
• MARKED						
• UNMARKED						
BROOD						
• EGGS						
• LARVAE						
• CAPPED						
QUEEN CELLS						
• SUPERCEDURE						
• SWARM						
FOOD						
• UNCAPPED HONEY						
• # CAPPED HONEY FRAMES						
• POLLEN						
PESTS						
• VARROA						
• WAX MOTHS						
TEMPERAMENT						
• CALM						
• AGGRESSIVE						
POPULATION						
• LOW						
• THRIVING						
• HIGH						
YIELD						

BEEHIVE INSPECTION

Date		Weather		Temperature	

	HIVE #1	HIVE #2	HIVE #3	HIVE #4	HIVE #5	NOTES
HIVE SIZE						
QUEEN						
• MARKED						
• UNMARKED						
BROOD						
• EGGS						
• LARVAE						
• CAPPED						
QUEEN CELLS						
• SUPERCEDURE						
• SWARM						
FOOD						
• UNCAPPED HONEY						
• # CAPPED HONEY FRAMES						
• POLLEN						
PESTS						
• VARROA						
• WAX MOTHS						
TEMPERAMENT						
• CALM						
• AGGRESSIVE						
POPULATION						
• LOW						
• THRIVING						
• HIGH						
YIELD						

BEEHIVE INSPECTION

Date		Weather		Temperature	

	HIVE #1	HIVE #2	HIVE #3	HIVE #4	HIVE #5	NOTES
HIVE SIZE						
QUEEN						
• MARKED						
• UNMARKED						
BROOD						
• EGGS						
• LARVAE						
• CAPPED						
QUEEN CELLS						
• SUPERCEDURE						
• SWARM						
FOOD						
• UNCAPPED HONEY						
• # CAPPED HONEY FRAMES						
• POLLEN						
PESTS						
• VARROA						
• WAX MOTHS						
TEMPERAMENT						
• CALM						
• AGGRESSIVE						
POPULATION						
• LOW						
• THRIVING						
• HIGH						
YIELD						

BEEHIVE INSPECTION

Date		Weather		Temperature	

	HIVE #1	HIVE #2	HIVE #3	HIVE #4	HIVE #5	NOTES
HIVE SIZE						
QUEEN						
• MARKED						
• UNMARKED						
BROOD						
• EGGS						
• LARVAE						
• CAPPED						
QUEEN CELLS						
• SUPERCEDURE						
• SWARM						
FOOD						
• UNCAPPED HONEY						
• # CAPPED HONEY FRAMES						
• POLLEN						
PESTS						
• VARROA						
• WAX MOTHS						
TEMPERAMENT						
• CALM						
• AGGRESSIVE						
POPULATION						
• LOW						
• THRIVING						
• HIGH						
YIELD						

BEEHIVE INSPECTION

Date		Weather		Temperature	

	HIVE #1	HIVE #2	HIVE #3	HIVE #4	HIVE #5	NOTES
HIVE SIZE						
QUEEN						
• MARKED						
• UNMARKED						
BROOD						
• EGGS						
• LARVAE						
• CAPPED						
QUEEN CELLS						
• SUPERCEDURE						
• SWARM						
FOOD						
• UNCAPPED HONEY						
• # CAPPED HONEY FRAMES						
• POLLEN						
PESTS						
• VARROA						
• WAX MOTHS						
TEMPERAMENT						
• CALM						
• AGGRESSIVE						
POPULATION						
• LOW						
• THRIVING						
• HIGH						
YIELD						

BEEHIVE INSPECTION

Date		Weather		Temperature	

	HIVE #1	HIVE #2	HIVE #3	HIVE #4	HIVE #5	NOTES
HIVE SIZE						
QUEEN						
• MARKED						
• UNMARKED						
BROOD						
• EGGS						
• LARVAE						
• CAPPED						
QUEEN CELLS						
• SUPERCEDURE						
• SWARM						
FOOD						
• UNCAPPED HONEY						
• # CAPPED HONEY FRAMES						
• POLLEN						
PESTS						
• VARROA						
• WAX MOTHS						
TEMPERAMENT						
• CALM						
• AGGRESSIVE						
POPULATION						
• LOW						
• THRIVING						
• HIGH						
YIELD						

MARKET DAYS

# MARKET PLANNER

DATE/S	MARKET	LOCATION	CONTACT	STALL BOOKED

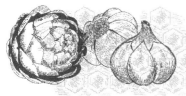

MARKET PREPARATION

MARKET		DATE/S			
ITEM	TO DO		COSTS		DONE

MARKET INVENTORY
& PRICE LIST

MARKET			DATE/S	
CUT FLOWERS	**PRICE**	**SEEDLINGS**		**PRICE**
HERBS		**VEGETABLES**		
FRUIT		**EGGS**		
HONEY		**OTHER**		
		WAX CANDLES		
		PRESERVES		

 # MARKET SALES

MARKET			DATE/S	
ITEM	**QTY**	**UNIT PRICE**		**AMOUNT**	
		TOTAL SALES			
		LESS EXPENSES			
		PROFIT / LOSS			

 # MARKET PLANNER

DATE/S	MARKET	LOCATION	CONTACT	STALL BOOKED

MARKET PREPARATION

MARKET		DATE/S			
ITEM	**TO DO**	**COSTS**		**DONE**	

MARKET INVENTORY & PRICE LIST

MARKET		DATE/S	

CUT FLOWERS	PRICE	SEEDLINGS	PRICE

HERBS		VEGETABLES	

FRUIT		EGGS	

HONEY		OTHER	
		WAX CANDLES	
		PRESERVES	

MARKET SALES

MARKET			DATE/S	
ITEM	**QTY**	**UNIT PRICE**		**AMOUNT**
		TOTAL SALES		
		LESS EXPENSES		
		PROFIT / LOSS		

 # MARKET PLANNER

DATE/S	MARKET	LOCATION	CONTACT	STALL BOOKED

MARKET
PREPARATION

MARKET		DATE/S	
ITEM	**TO DO**	**COSTS**		**DONE**

MARKET INVENTORY & PRICE LIST

MARKET			DATE/S	

CUT FLOWERS	PRICE		SEEDLINGS	PRICE

HERBS			VEGETABLES	

FRUIT			EGGS	

HONEY			OTHER	
			WAX CANDLES	
			PRESERVES	

 # MARKET SALES

MARKET			DATE/S		
ITEM		QTY	UNIT PRICE		AMOUNT
		TOTAL SALES			
		LESS EXPENSES			
		PROFIT / LOSS			

 # MARKET PLANNER

DATE/S	MARKET	LOCATION	CONTACT	STALL BOOKED

MARKET
PREPARATION

MARKET		DATE/S	

ITEM	TO DO	COSTS		DONE

MARKET INVENTORY
& PRICE LIST

MARKET		DATE/S	

CUT FLOWERS	PRICE	SEEDLINGS	PRICE
HERBS		VEGETABLES	
FRUIT		EGGS	
HONEY		OTHER	
		WAX CANDLES	
		PRESERVES	

MARKET SALES

MARKET			DATE/S	
ITEM	**QTY**	**UNIT PRICE**		**AMOUNT**
		TOTAL SALES		
		LESS EXPENSES		
		PROFIT / LOSS		

 # MARKET PLANNER

DATE/S	MARKET	LOCATION	CONTACT	STALL BOOKED

MARKET
PREPARATION

MARKET		DATE/S		
ITEM	TO DO	COSTS		DONE

MARKET INVENTORY
& PRICE LIST

MARKET			DATE/S	

CUT FLOWERS	PRICE		SEEDLINGS	PRICE

HERBS			VEGETABLES	

FRUIT			EGGS	

HONEY			OTHER	
			WAX CANDLES	
			PRESERVES	

MARKET SALES

MARKET			DATE/S	
ITEM	**QTY**	**UNIT PRICE**		**AMOUNT**
		TOTAL SALES		
		LESS EXPENSES		
		PROFIT / LOSS		

 # MARKET PLANNER

DATE/S	MARKET	LOCATION	CONTACT	STALL BOOKED

MARKET
PREPARATION

MARKET		DATE/S		
ITEM	TO DO	COSTS		DONE

MARKET INVENTORY
& PRICE LIST

MARKET		DATE/S	

CUT FLOWERS	PRICE	SEEDLINGS	PRICE
HERBS		VEGETABLES	
FRUIT		EGGS	
HONEY		OTHER	
		WAX CANDLES	
		PRESERVES	

MARKET SALES

MARKET		DATE/S		
ITEM	**QTY**	**UNIT PRICE**		**AMOUNT**	
		TOTAL SALES			
		LESS EXPENSES			
		PROFIT / LOSS			

MARKET PLANNER

DATE/S	MARKET	LOCATION	CONTACT	STALL BOOKED

MARKET
PREPARATION

MARKET		DATE/S			
ITEM	TO DO		COSTS		DONE

MARKET INVENTORY
& PRICE LIST

MARKET			DATE/S	

CUT FLOWERS	PRICE		SEEDLINGS	PRICE

HERBS			VEGETABLES	

FRUIT			EGGS	

HONEY			OTHER	
			WAX CANDLES	
			PRESERVES	

 # MARKET SALES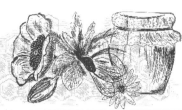

MARKET			DATE/S		
ITEM		QTY	UNIT PRICE	AMOUNT	
		TOTAL SALES			
		LESS EXPENSES			
		PROFIT / LOSS			

 # MARKET PLANNER

DATE/S	MARKET	LOCATION	CONTACT	STALL BOOKED

MARKET PREPARATION

MARKET		DATE/S		
ITEM	**TO DO**	**COSTS**		**DONE**

MARKET INVENTORY
& PRICE LIST

MARKET				DATE/S	

CUT FLOWERS	PRICE		SEEDLINGS	PRICE

HERBS			VEGETABLES	

FRUIT			EGGS	

HONEY			OTHER	
			WAX CANDLES	
			PRESERVES	

MARKET SALES

MARKET			DATE/S		
ITEM		**QTY**	**UNIT PRICE**		**AMOUNT**
		TOTAL SALES			
		LESS EXPENSES			
		PROFIT / LOSS			

 # MARKET PLANNER

DATE/S	MARKET	LOCATION	CONTACT	STALL BOOKED

MARKET PREPARATION

MARKET		DATE/S	

ITEM	TO DO	COSTS		DONE

MARKET INVENTORY
& PRICE LIST

MARKET		DATE/S	

CUT FLOWERS	PRICE	SEEDLINGS	PRICE

HERBS		VEGETABLES	

FRUIT		EGGS	

HONEY		OTHER	
		WAX CANDLES	
		PRESERVES	

MARKET SALES

MARKET			DATE/S		
ITEM		QTY	UNIT PRICE		AMOUNT
			TOTAL SALES		
			LESS EXPENSES		
			PROFIT / LOSS		

 # MARKET PLANNER

DATE/S	MARKET	LOCATION	CONTACT	STALL BOOKED

MARKET PREPARATION

MARKET		DATE/S	

ITEM	TO DO	COSTS		DONE

MARKET INVENTORY
& PRICE LIST

MARKET		DATE/S	

CUT FLOWERS	PRICE	SEEDLINGS	PRICE

HERBS		VEGETABLES	

FRUIT		EGGS	

HONEY		OTHER	
		WAX CANDLES	
		PRESERVES	

MARKET SALES

MARKET		DATE/S		
ITEM	**QTY**	**UNIT PRICE**		**AMOUNT**	
	TOTAL SALES				
	LESS EXPENSES				
	PROFIT / LOSS				

 # MARKET PLANNER

DATE/S	MARKET	LOCATION	CONTACT	STALL BOOKED

MARKET PREPARATION

MARKET		DATE/S		
ITEM	**TO DO**	**COSTS**		**DONE**

MARKET INVENTORY & PRICE LIST

MARKET			DATE/S	

CUT FLOWERS	PRICE		SEEDLINGS	PRICE

HERBS			VEGETABLES	

FRUIT			EGGS	

HONEY			OTHER	
			WAX CANDLES	
			PRESERVES	

MARKET SALES

MARKET			DATE/S	
ITEM	**QTY**	**UNIT PRICE**		**AMOUNT**
		TOTAL SALES		
		LESS EXPENSES		
		PROFIT / LOSS		

 # MARKET PLANNER

DATE/S	MARKET	LOCATION	CONTACT	STALL BOOKED

MARKET
PREPARATION

MARKET		DATE/S		
ITEM	**TO DO**	**COSTS**		**DONE**

MARKET INVENTORY
& PRICE LIST

MARKET		DATE/S	

CUT FLOWERS	PRICE	SEEDLINGS	PRICE
HERBS		**VEGETABLES**	
FRUIT		**EGGS**	
HONEY		**OTHER**	
		WAX CANDLES	
		PRESERVES	

 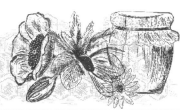

MARKET SALES

MARKET		DATE/S	

ITEM	QTY	UNIT PRICE		AMOUNT	
			TOTAL SALES		
			LESS EXPENSES		
			PROFIT / LOSS		

HOMESTEAD
CONTACTS

CONTACTS

NAME	ADDRESS	PHONE	EMAIL
A			
B			
C			

CONTACTS

NAME	ADDRESS	PHONE	EMAIL
D			
E			
F			

CONTACTS

NAME	ADDRESS	PHONE	EMAIL
G			
H			
I			

CONTACTS

NAME	ADDRESS	PHONE	EMAIL
J			
K			
L			

CONTACTS

NAME	ADDRESS	PHONE	EMAIL
M			
N			
O			

CONTACTS

NAME	ADDRESS	PHONE	EMAIL
PQ			
R			
S			

CONTACTS

NAME	ADDRESS	PHONE	EMAIL
T			
UV			
WXYZ			

CONTACTS

NAME	ADDRESS	PHONE	EMAIL

NOTES

Made in the USA
Monee, IL
21 November 2023

47060584R00176